Grammar and the
Teaching of Writing

Grammar and the Teaching of Writing

Limits and Possibilities

Rei R. Noguchi
California State University, Northridge

National Council of Teachers of English
1111 Kenyon Road, Urbana, Illinois 61801

Staff Editor: Rona S. Smith

Cover Design: Robin Loughran; computer image by Scott A. Burns

Interior Design: Tom Kovacs for TGK Design

NCTE Stock Number: 18747-3020

Library of Congress Cataloging-in-Publication Data

Noguchi, Rei R.
    Grammar and the teaching of writing : Limits and possibilities / Rei R. Noguchi.
      p. cm.
    Includes bibliographical references.
    ISBN 0-8141-1874-7
    1. English language—Rhetoric—Study and teaching. 2. English language—Composition and exercises—Study and teaching. 3. English language—Grammar—Study and teaching. I. Title.
PE1404.N64   1991
808'.042'07—dc20   90-26616
                                     CIP

Contents

Preface

Grammar and writing have been, at best, uncomfortable partners in most programs designed to improve compositional skills, not just in developmental writing programs at colleges but also and, perhaps more extensively, in language arts programs in the elementary and secondary schools. For many students, the formal study of grammar seems far removed from their daily use of language, cut off from the spontaneity and verve they so often demonstrate in the give-and-take of everyday conversation. It is no secret that students chafe at learning the numerous abstract and often arcane grammatical categories and the almost equally opaque "rules of grammar." They chafe most, perhaps, at the seemingly endless—and often mindless—drills and exercises designed to promote acquisition of the entire grammatical apparatus presumably needed for writing improvement.

If many students grow to dislike grammar, many teachers view formal grammar instruction as a necessary ingredient in writing improvement. Others, much more begrudgingly, view it as a necessary evil. For the latter group of teachers, grammar instruction enters into writing instruction either because the curriculum mandates it (usually enforced by the use of standardized tests) or because teachers have nothing better to offer in its place. Whether teachers in the latter two situations believe in the value of formal grammar instruction or not, they, like most of their students, look with apprehension at the formidable and time-consuming undertaking with each new class. For those teachers who view the study of grammar as a necessary accompaniment to writing instruction, grammar is taught primarily because of a staunch belief that a knowledge of it improves writing quality. Yet this belief has increasingly come under attack from researchers in the field of composition, whose findings indicate that the formal study of grammar brings no significant gains to students' writing and, indeed, may have a deleterious effect on writing by taking away classroom time that might be better spent on more productive kinds of activities.

With the foregoing as both guide and incentive, this study has three principal aims:

1. To reduce the breadth of formal grammar instruction by first locating those areas where grammar and writing overlap and then identifying those kinds of writing problems most amenable to treatment with a grammar-based approach.

2. To decrease the classroom hours spent on formal grammar instruction by showing how to capitalize on the already-acquired yet unconscious knowledge that all native writers have of their language.

3. To make this streamlined "writer's grammar" more productive by showing how to integrate it with style, content, and organization.

The overall aim is to make more time available for other writing activities by making less grammar do more. With such aims, this book is directed not towards grammar teachers who teach grammar solely as an academic discipline but specifically towards teachers of writing who, to varying degrees, struggle with the unwieldy partnership of grammar and writing.

The study itself comprises six chapters. Chapters 1 and 2 serve several ends: to examine some probable reasons why grammar instruction has failed to improve writing quality, to delimit radically the scope of grammar instruction, and to identify specific areas where a knowledge of a minimal set of grammatical categories might be of help. Chapters 3 and 4 focus on the use of native-speaker abilities in place of formal grammar instruction to treat certain kinds of sentence-level writing problems. Chapter 5 continues with the method outlined in Chapters 3 and 4 but also suggests a promising way to integrate the diminished focus on grammar with style, content, and organization. Finally, Chapter 6 summarizes several "pragmatic paradoxes" that currently beset grammar instruction in the schools.

I wish to thank the School of Humanities of California State University, Northridge, for providing course-release time to complete part of the research in this study and California State University, Northridge, for providing a much welcomed respite in the form of a sabbatical leave to transfer thoughts from mind to computer screen to paper, though not always in that order.

1 The Limits of Grammar in Writing Improvement

Since its incorporation into American classrooms in the latter half of the eighteenth century, formal instruction in English grammar has always had a place in the school curriculum. Indeed, for many teachers, the subject of grammar seems to evoke something basic and intrinsic to American education itself. Thus, at a time when much new and sometimes even faddish material has entered the curriculum, many teachers still devote a considerable number of classroom hours to "old-fashioned" grammar instruction—that is, the parts of speech and the structure and functions of various syntactic constructions (e.g., phrases, clauses, and sentences), with accompanying advice on usage. Although the rationale for formal grammar instruction lies partly in a historical tradition dating back ultimately to the classical trivium of grammar, logic, and rhetoric, it also lies in more immediate and practical matters, specifically, the improvement of language skills, particularly writing skills. Indeed, the connection between grammar and writing has been so strongly ingrained in teachers that many believe instruction in formal grammar enhances, even ensures, the development of good writing. Yet in the last half century or so, this belief has come increasingly under fire. Critics contend that formal grammar instruction fails to produce any significant improvement in student writing and, worse yet, consumes valuable classroom hours that could be spent on more fruitful matters. To staunch pro-grammar advocates, the charge seems either outright heresy or part of the latest teaching fad; to the anti-grammar advocates, it is the clarion call for a more efficient and productive language arts curriculum. Yet how justified is the criticism of formal grammar instruction? Is grammar really worth teaching and learning? To answer this question and ultimately to address the role of grammar in the schools—if any—we need to examine more closely just where grammar has apparently failed and why.

For purposes of discussion, I use the term "grammar" narrowly here. Although the ensuing discussion also has relevance to structural and transformational/generative grammar, I restrict the term (at least initially) to traditional grammar since this type of grammar is the one most commonly taught in the classroom. Second, within traditional grammar, I restrict the term to mean the set of categories, functions, and rules (both descriptive and prescriptive) that teachers commonly employ to describe a sentence and its parts. (As we shall see later in Chapter 3, this traditional—indeed, popular—notion of grammar contrasts sharply with the transformational/generative notion of grammar as a native speaker's unconscious underlying knowledge of his or her language.) Teachers of traditional grammar, when analyzing sentences, employ such categories as noun, verb, phrase, and clause and such functions as subject, direct object, and predicate nominative. They use such rules as "A sentence is composed of a subject and a predicate" or "An article precedes a noun in sequence" (two descriptive rules), and "Never use the word *ain't*" or "Never end a sentence with a preposition" (two prescriptive rules, or rules of usage). I use the phrase "formal grammar instruction" to mean the direct and sustained teaching of these categories, functions, and rules through definition, drill, and exercises.

The Research

Although studies questioning the value of formal grammar instruction for improving writing occur in print as early as Hoyt's 1906 study, such studies have appeared in increasing numbers in the last half of this century. A sampling includes studies by DeBoer (1959), Meckel (1963), Elley et al. (1976), Sutton (1976), Falk (1979), Tabbert (1984), Hartwell (1985), and Sanborn (1986). A few studies defend the study of formal grammar (e.g., Neuleib 1977; Kolln 1981; Holt 1982; Davis 1984; Neuleib and Brosnahan 1987), but anti-grammar studies have, by far, outnumbered the pro-grammar ones. Braddock et al. (1963) summarize and assess such studies from 1957 to 1963; Hillocks (1986) does the same from 1967 to 1986. The conclusions of Braddock et al. and of Hillocks are both highly critical of formal grammar instruction in the schools. Braddock et al. baldly state:

> In view of the widespread agreement of research studies based upon many types of students and teachers, the conclusion can be stated in strong and unqualified terms: the teaching of formal grammar has a negligible or, because it usually displaces some instruction and practice in actual composition, even a harmful effect on the improvement of writing. (37–38)

Kolln, in her defense of grammar instruction, charges that the Braddock study is flawed by excessive reliance on studies which lacked experimental control. This same charge, however, is less applicable to the Hillocks study. Eliminating the studies flawed by inadequate research design and using sophisticated statistical "meta-analyses" of previous studies, Hillocks also reaches harsh criticism of formal grammar instruction, particularly formal instruction in traditional grammar. He writes:

> The study of traditional school grammar (i.e., the definition of parts of speech, the parsing of sentences, etc.) has no effect on raising the quality of student writing. Every other focus of instruction examined in this review is stronger. Taught in certain ways, grammar and mechanics instruction has a deleterious effect on student writing. In some studies a heavy emphasis on mechanics and usage (e.g., marking every error) resulted in significant losses in overall quality. School boards, administrators, and teachers who impose the systematic study of traditional school grammar on their students over lengthy periods of time in the name of teaching writing do them a gross disservice which should not be tolerated by anyone concerned with the effective teaching of good writing. We need to learn how to teach standard usage and mechanics after careful task analysis and with minimal grammar. (248–49)

While comprehensive and careful studies such as Hillocks's add more credence to the claim that formal grammar instruction fails to improve writing, both the individual and composite studies leave unanswered several important and intriguing questions. Assuming that such studies are valid and reliable, *why* does formal instruction in grammar fail to produce any significant improvement in writing quality? Is the failure due to the very nature of the approach—in which case there is something inherently defective in the approach itself and, hence, little or no possibility of success—or is the failure due to the way grammar has been taught (in which case there exists an increased possibility for success)? Besides ignoring such questions, the studies cited above also tend to generalize too quickly from part to whole. Just because formal instruction in grammar proves generally unproductive in improving writing does not necessarily mean that we should discard all aspects of grammar instruction. Stated in a slightly different way, is the whole approach irrelevant (and therefore unproductive) or just parts of it? Could it be that the larger failures of the irrelevant parts have hidden or devalued the benefits of the relevant parts? Could it even be that the relevant parts of the approach have failed because we have implemented them in the wrong way? I believe these kinds of questions need answers lest we sound—indeed, encourage—too hastily and perhaps unjustly the doom of all grammar instruction in the schools, both traditional and nontraditional, formal and informal.

The Failure of Grammar Instruction: Probable Causes

The reason formal grammar instruction has generally proved ineffective in improving writing probably lies in several complex and interrelated causes. Although these causes are often difficult to separate from one another, the most likely ones can be conveniently summarized as follows:

1. Formal grammar, being uninteresting or too difficult, is not adequately learned by students.
2. Formal grammar, even if adequately learned, is not transferred to writing situations.
3. Formal grammar, even if adequately learned, is not transferable to writing situations.

Teachers, especially those who have struggled in presenting traditional grammar as a means of improving writing, will readily agree that Causes 1–3 are highly plausible. Cause 1 assumes that because of a lack of interest or because of the difficulty of the subject matter itself, students simply fail to learn formal grammar or at least fail to learn it to a degree sufficient to apply it effectively to writing. Causes 2 and 3 are similar in that they both assume that students have acquired a sufficient knowledge of formal grammar; however, Cause 2 assumes that students fail to apply that knowledge to relevant writing situations because they are neglectful, while Cause 3 assumes that students fail to apply the knowledge because that knowledge is irrelevant to writing situations. Although there may be other contributing factors, Causes 1–3 seem to be the most prominent in the alleged failure of formal grammar instruction to improve writing. If so, it is worthwhile to examine these causes more closely, starting with the more obvious ones.

Cause 1: Grammar Is Not Adequately Learned

With respect to Cause 1 (i.e., formal grammar, being too difficult or too uninteresting, is not adequately learned), several things are certain. All will agree that students who do not acquire a body of knowledge cannot apply it. Moreover, there is much evidence to show that student interest in a subject facilitates the learning of the subject. Unfortunately, formal instruction in grammar has, for the most part, proved uninteresting for students. With the exception of those few students who willingly and enthusiastically engage in any kind of academic pursuit, most students find the formal study of grammar, at best, dry and, at worst, tedious and boring. Such sentiments are not without cause if we consider the usual way grammar has been presented—the item-by-item definitions of the syntactic categories, the rote memorization of constructions and their patterns, the seemingly endless drills and exercises. It is no wonder that many students end up hating grammar with a passion nor that the general populace comes to perceive grammar, in the words of W. Nelson Francis, as an academic subject "fit for only those in whose veins the red blood of life has long since turned to ink" (1954, 299).

Though influential, the lack of student interest in grammar cannot be the sole and certainly not the root cause for the failure of formal grammar instruction. Many teachers have sought to make and, indeed, have succeeded in making grammar instruction more interesting, as witnessed by the numerous methods and tips that have been disseminated in journals, newsletters, and teacher conferences, not to mention by word of mouth. It is also worth noting here that students often find subjects other than grammar uninteresting (proverbially, math); yet, these students acquire enough knowledge through formal instruction to profit in applied fields. Moreover, we sometimes find students who develop an interest, even an avid one, in the formal study of grammar but whose quality of writing is not commensurate with this interest. Conversely, we often find students who show little or no interest in the formal study of grammar yet who write well, some, very well. We must conclude that while the lack of interest in grammar is probably a contributing cause to the failure of formal grammar instruction, it is not the chief one.

An underlying cause may be the difficulty of grammar itself. What makes traditional grammar so difficult for students seems to lie in its abstractness and its impreciseness. The impreciseness stems in part from the fact that the eighteenth-century grammarians sometimes forced English (a Germanic language) into categories designed for Latin (a Romance language). The fit has never been comfortable, especially for students, who wonder why the verb in *I start my new job tomorrow* is classified as present tense even though it involves a future event or, more generally, why English has inflectional endings for present and past tense but none for the so-called future tense. The impreciseness becomes even more problematic in the notional definitions used to define the various syntactic categories. Thus, students puzzle over—and teachers labor to explain—why a sequence of words such as *Because I want a Beatles album* is not a sentence even though it represents a "complete thought" or why a word can sometimes take the form of a verb but function as a noun yet not be "a person, place, or thing" (as in *Winning is nice*). More difficult for students to accommodate, however, has been the abstractness of grammar study itself. Frustrated students frequently complain that studying grammar is like studying math. Yet, in some ways, formal grammar is more frustrating to students because it seems so remote from their own everyday language experience. Although the study of formal grammar can have a concrete side (i.e., working with actual samples of written or spoken English), it also has a prominent and, as some would claim, an overabundant abstract side. This other side deals, of course, with the "metalanguage" of grammar, the language used to describe grammar. Thus, in order to help students analyze the structure of English, teachers spend many classroom hours introducing the abstract technical vocabulary of grammatical analysis, for example, "subject," "predicate," "prepositional phrase," "relative clause," "nominative absolute," and the various rules associated with these constructs. While students can utter, write, hear, and understand a "sentence" (the latter term itself being a part of the metalanguage), they do not so easily perceive the abstract concepts used to categorize the various parts and patterns of the sentence.

The abstraction involved in grammar study may help explain why students find grammar difficult (and also, perhaps, uninteresting) to learn and, ultimately, why formal instruction adds little to writing improvement. Put in more general terms, if a body of knowledge is too difficult to learn, it obviously will not be learned, and if it is not learned, it obviously cannot be applied successfully. Yet, as plausible as this chain of reasoning appears, it does not explain some commonly observed facts. Although some teachers, to buttress their support of direct grammar instruction, will claim that their best writers have a solid knowledge of formal grammar, there are also students who know little or no formal grammar but who, nevertheless, write well, sometimes even better than students with a knowledge of formal grammar. Nor does the reasoning above explain why increased doses of grammar instruction fail to produce a corresponding degree of writing improvement. Given these observed facts, we can say that formal grammar instruction may bear some relationship to writing improvement, but the relationship is not a direct one.

Though generally pessimistic, the foregoing conclusion does leave some room for optimism. The above conclusion does not, for example, preclude the possibility that some students can benefit from a knowledge of formal grammar. While it may be that not all students benefit directly (or indirectly) from formal grammar instruction, some students may. If so, it would be reasonable to argue that if more of these students learned formal grammar adequately, perhaps they would benefit more in their writing.

Cause 2: Grammar Is Not Transferred to Writing Situations

Following the present line of argument, let us assume that instruction in grammar has been successfully implemented; that is, students are sufficiently equipped to apply formal grammar to their writing. Will this ensure that writing improvement will follow? Not necessarily so. One way that formal grammar instruction can still fail is that students, though possessing sufficient knowledge of formal grammar, fail to apply that knowledge to their writing. This situation seems highly likely because we are all well aware of cases where people who have acquired knowledge in one domain do not transfer that knowledge, even though it is possible to do so, to other domains. Could it also be so with the formal knowledge of grammar and the practical skill of writing? Certainly, there are many plausible psychological reasons why this transfer does not take place, from inattentiveness or carelessness, to ignorance of the applicability of grammatical knowledge, to sheer laziness. If the explanation that students acquire a sufficient knowledge of formal grammar but fail to apply it is correct, then it seems that harsh criticism of grammar instruction has not been entirely fair. That is, the fault may lie not in the approach, but in a failure to apply the approach in the appropriate writing situations. Although this does not explain why students who have little or no knowledge of formal grammar sometimes write well, it may to some extent explain why students who have mastered formal grammar fail to demonstrate a parallel improvement in their writing, at least in those areas where a knowledge of formal grammar is directly relevant.

If the foregoing is true, then we cannot so easily and so assuredly dismiss all formal grammar instruction. If grammar instruction can potentially improve writing, but students, for whatever reason, do not apply their learning of formal grammar, then the failure is not so much of the method but of our failure to instill the importance of proper revising or proofreading. We cannot blame the method if it is never implemented. As with any potentially beneficial method, the same warning holds: "Use it or lose it." This point becomes especially significant when we consider that most anti-grammar studies fail not only to verify if grammar was learned to a sufficient degree to apply (i.e., Cause 1) but also, and more important, to ascertain whether the knowledge of formal grammar was applied at all in the writing process (i.e., Cause 2). Though these researchers frequently take pains to verify that instruction in grammar took place, they fail to ascertain whether this instruction was successful and, just as important, whether it was actually implemented in the revising or proofreading stage. It is also worth pointing out that the problem of nonapplication of a body of knowledge is not just a problem afflicting a knowledge of grammar but one afflicting all knowledge related to writing. Writing teachers, for example, often offer explicit instruction in content, organization, tone, and many other things which presumably enhance writing quality, but this instruction, too, as witnessed by the many imperfect essays turned in by students, is often not transferred to actual writing. If the problem of transfer is a general one and not restricted to grammar alone, it seems unfair in principle to castigate, not to mention, banish, one realm of knowledge and not all the others. Cause 2 (i.e., that formal grammar has failed because it is not transferred to writing), if applicable, offers a modicum of hope for advocates of formal grammar instruction.

Cause 3: Grammar Is Not Transferable to Writing Situations

While Cause 2 leaves some room for optimism, Cause 3 (i.e., that formal grammar has failed because it comprises a body of knowledge which is not transferable to writing situations) is, if true, decidedly fatal. I say "fatal" because, if Cause 3 is true, no matter how thoroughly and carefully instructors teach grammar, no matter how thoroughly and carefully students study and learn grammar, and no matter how thoroughly and carefully they apply that knowledge to writing, the efforts are, by necessity, doomed to fail. The failure in this case would result not from personal lapses on the part of teachers or students but rather from the brute fact that the domain of grammar does not overlap in any significant way with the domain of writing, or put more simply, formal grammar has no real connection with writing.

The Connection between Grammar and Writing

Just what connection, if any, *does* grammar have with writing? To answer this, we need to identify clearly those areas of grammar and writing which overlap. This is crucial because if writing comprises mainly areas which do not overlap with grammar—as the anti-grammar critics have implied—teachers would do well to retire their well-worn grammar texts and teach other means of writing improvement. However, if overlap does exist, teachers might be inspired to continue, but more important, they might be inspired to focus grammar instruction specifically on the overlapping areas. Subdividing writing into the more-or-less traditional areas of content (invention), organization (arrangement), and style (which includes mechanics and punctuation) reveals more clearly the areas in which a knowledge of formal grammar can and cannot help.

Grammar and Content

Formal grammar cannot help, at least not directly, in the area of content. "Content" involves cognitive meaning, or, here, the basic idea or ideas that the writer wants to convey. Although there is some controversy on whether or not content can actually be separated from form, it is important to stress that grammar instruction has traditionally made that separation. That is, when teachers teach grammar formally, they focus on the identification, organization, and functions of the various syntactic constructions with respect to one another, but usually not on the semantic content of these constructions. Put in another way, formal grammar instruction generally focuses on structures and their relationships, not meaning and meaning relationships. By separating content from form, we, of course, make talking about form easier. Thus we talk of the classification of verbs into transitive, intransitive, and linking verbs, or the arrangement of certain grammatical functions like subject, verb, and direct object in a sentence, without having to discuss the individual and composite meanings of the syntactic constructs. The focus on form comes about partly through academic training and partly through pedagogical necessity since teachers usually know much more about the analysis of syntactic forms than the analysis of meaning. We can summarize here by generalizing that because formal grammar, as commonly taught, deals with the structure of sentences and its parts and not with the semantic content of these structures, it cannot help students improve or generate content. Although sentences offer a form—or perhaps better, a means—to convey content, a knowledge of sentence structure can offer no help if writers have little, no, or inappropriate content to convey. When students relate that they have "nothing to say" in their writing, the remedy lies not in more grammar instruction but rather in activities such as brainstorming, group discussion, interviewing, or library research, all of which can be and, indeed, are best conducted without recourse to formal grammar.

Grammar and Organization

If formal grammar has to do with form and not with content *per se*, we might think that instruction in formal grammar might be helpful in improving organization, particularly since organization concerns the arrangement of both form and content. While we usually talk of the organization of ideas, it also seems plausible to talk about the organization of forms. For example, essays can be said to exhibit various arrangements of form, just as sentences themselves have various arrangements. The key question here, of course is, does the arrangement or organization of sentences contribute to the arrangement or organization of essays? One line of thinking goes, if grammar has to do with the structure of sentences and if sentences make up an essay, shouldn't the knowledge of sentence structure aid the writer in organizing an essay? Stated in a slightly different way, shouldn't the sum of the structure of the parts (i.e., sentences) equal the structure of the whole (i.e., the essay)? Unfortunately, this chain of reasoning does not hold for at least two reasons. First, essays are organized not just by form but also by meaning. In a narrative essay, for example, we usually organize events according to time; in an argumentative essay, we often organize arguments from weakest to strongest for a climactic effect. As suggested earlier, however, formal grammar instruction rarely focuses on the organization of meaning, let alone the organization of these kinds of meaning. Even if we assume that an essay is organized strictly on the basis of form, a knowledge of sentence structure still cannot help in organizing the essay. This is so because the organization of an essay, among other things, involves arrangement of units larger than the sentence (e.g., paragraphs) and, within paragraphs, the sequential organization of one sentence to the next, the "connectedness" of sentences. Sentence structure, however, deals with the organization of form only *within* the sentence, not between and among sentences. Although a knowledge of formal grammar may enlighten students on how forms are organized inside a sentence, it will not shed light on how one sentence is sequenced with respect to another and still another in a paragraph or essay. Given such facts, we can conclude that the structure of a sentence and an essay (or paragraph) differ not only in breadth but also in kind. Even though sentences can be said to comprise an essay, it does not necessarily follow that the structure of the parts is equivalent to the structure of the whole. Just as we would not claim that a knowledge of the structure of words enhances a knowledge of the structure of sentences, so we should not—and cannot—claim that a knowledge of the structure of sentences enhances a knowledge of the structure of essays.

Grammar and Style

While formal grammar instruction seems to offer little in the area of essay organization, it does seem more potentially beneficial in the area of style. "Style" here is used broadly to encompass characteristic or recurrent linguistic features. Style includes not only syntactic and morphological forms but also salient features of punctuation and spelling. Just as syntactic and morphological forms can help delineate the style of written texts, so too can features of punctuation and spelling. Thus we can speak of recurrent or characteristic features of punctuation (e.g., unconventional use of commas) or recurrent or characteristic features of spelling (e.g., use of phonetic spellings). Because style involves both standard and nonstandard features, it covers such aspects of "mechanics" as verb tense, sentence fragments, run-ons, comma splices, and subject-verb agreement. But it also covers more than mechanics insofar as it also deals with options that lead to effective communication of content (e.g., the sequencing of linguistic elements, parallelism, subordination, transitions, and pronoun reference). Given such territory, formal grammar instruction seems especially promising for several reasons. For one, style, like grammar, typically has to do with form or, at least, can be viewed with respect to form. Thus we can speak of style as a recurrent or characteristic choice of form. Second, style can be studied with respect to sentences; that is, we can speak of a style of sentences. Certainly we can say that Hemingway's or Faulkner's sentences have a characteristic form, or style. Third, the style of sentences can and does contribute significantly to the overall style of an essay; that is, there is considerable overlap between cumulative effects of sentence style and the overall style of an essay. Hence it is not only possible but also common to analyze the style of an essay in terms of its component sentences. We can, for instance, get at the writing style of Hemingway or Faulkner by examining the style of their sentences. Last and more pragmatic, style is an area in which many of the technical concepts introduced in formal grammar instruction become descriptively relevant. We can analyze student writing to discover that some write with a "nominal" style (*The utilization of computers for the task was a decision of the planners*) while others write with a "verbal" style (*The planners decided to utilize computers for the task*); we can talk of students writing with a "coordinate" style, with many sentences joined by coordinating conjunctions, while others write with a "subordinate" style, with many embedded elements. In sum, of the three traditional areas of writing, formal instruction in grammar has potentially the most to offer in the area of style. For the other two areas (organization and content), formal grammar instruction, at least as it is currently practiced, cannot bring any significant benefit. Indeed, the inability of formal grammar to contribute anything useful to content and organization explains why grammar cannot serve as a comprehensive approach to writing. Stated in terms of Cause 3 (as discussed earlier), formal grammar, even if learned adequately, is not transferable to essay organization and content but is potentially transferable to the area of style.

If grammar is potentially transferable to style and if Causes 1 and 2 are negated in some way, then formal instruction in grammar can be of help in the area of style. For example, students can apply their formal knowledge of "subject" and "verb" to detect and identify errors in number agreement, their formal knowledge of "passive sentence" to avoid its overuse, or their formal knowledge of "restrictive relative clause" and "nonrestrictive relative clause" to check for comma errors.

The Relative Importance of Style to Writing Quality

Just because formal grammar overlaps significantly with style, however, does not necessarily mean that formal instruction in grammar belongs in the school curriculum. For example, it could be that style is not as crucial to writing quality as are organization and content, or that style could be enhanced by means other than formal grammar instruction. There is no question that content and organization play a crucial role in writing quality. Indeed, it would be somewhat bizarre for teachers to claim that a student's writing was competent but that it was deficient in content or organization. However, it seems less strange for teachers to claim that a student's writing was competent but deficient in style. This suggests, at least to a considerable number of teachers, that style may not play as crucial a role in writing quality as do content and organization. While I believe this to be essentially true, we should not discount the importance of style in writing.

In at least two ways, style has been given too little emphasis and, at least in one way, too much emphasis. First, style is often narrowly and wrongly viewed as a kind of embellishment that writers add to sentences. That is, content and organization are viewed as primary, with style a mere cosmetic. Writers can add it here, remove it there, presumably without greatly affecting the quality of the writing. Given such a view, style seems something extra and very minor compared to content and organization. This, of course, leads to the untenable conclusion that there exists a "styleless," or completely neutral way of writing. A neutral style, however, is still a style. Even if we grant the false assumption that style is mere embellishment, it would, nonetheless, be an ingredient that can affect every sentence in the text. This means that style is just as global, or all-encompassing, as organization and content, and, therefore, that lapses in style can be just as pervasive as lapses in organization and content. Second, style is not something completely isolated from content and organization, but something which interacts with both. With respect to content, we can speak of stylistic differences between, for example, *used car* and *pre-owned car*. Although both expressions refer to a car that was previously owned and driven by someone else, the choice will affect meaning since *used car* and *pre-owned car* differ in connotation. With respect to organization, both *the frightened man* (as in *The frightened man ran away*) and *the man frightened* (as in *The man frightened ran away*) refer to a man instilled with fear; however, the two expressions have slightly different meanings because of the different sequential organization of the adjective and noun. (The first expression focuses more on fear as an inner experience while the second expression focuses more on the act of frightening.)

If classroom instruction has given too little attention to the interaction of style with content and organization, it also has probably given too much emphasis to just one aspect of style, namely, sentence mechanics. Here, misconceptions have led to extremes by both anti- and pro-grammar teachers. For both groups, the extremes stem ultimately from viewing style primarily—or sometimes, exclusively—as matters of mechanics—for example, sentencing errors, punctuation, and spelling. On one extreme, we find a staunch cadre of pro-grammar instructors who place so much emphasis on the mechanical errors that they "red-ink" student writing to a fatal hemorrhage and thereby destroy student interest in writing and writing improvement. These instructors, who exemplify hard-line traditional grammar teaching at its worst, are, fortunately, decreasing in number; yet their influence remains strong at all levels of formal education. At the other extreme, we find a growing number of equally staunch anti-grammar teachers who view mechanical errors as unimportant low-level "surface" features which detract little from writing quality and which students can easily edit out during the writing process. These hard-liners forego any kind of grammar instruction, and many believe that students will eventually outgrow mechanical errors on the presumption that, as students increase their reading and writing experience, they will correct all the errors on their own.

I believe the hard-line anti-grammar teachers with their reluctance to address such errors in a systematic way are just as misguided and self-defeating as the hard-line pro-grammar teachers who address them with overexuberance. What seems lost in these internecine battles is the middle ground. For example, mechanical errors cannot be as trivial as the hard-line anti-grammar teachers make them out to be. Though certainly surface errors, these unconventional features ought not to be deemed simply "unimportant" (and, therefore, best ignored), since many readers, particularly in business and other professional settings, perceive them as prime indicators of poor writing. While classroom teachers may overlook these unconventional features as minor in comparison to errors in content and organization, this is not so with most of the educated reading public, which, fairly or unfairly, perceives such features as major improprieties. (I am reminded here of a native English student, who, oblivious to the strength of such reader perceptions, wrote in a semester-end course evaluation, "I learned alot about english grammer.") If good writing results, as we teach our students, from a reader-based perspective rather than from a writer-based one, then, from the eyes of the reading public, the unconventional features may not only distract but also detract from writing quality. Second, such features are not so easily edited out during the rewriting process as the anti-grammar teachers claim. The problem here is that, if students do not recognize the unconventional features as unconventional, they cannot edit them out. (That students today are generally less familiar with the conventions of writing because they do less outside reading only exacerbates the problem.) The persistence of unconventional writing features well into the college years and even beyond suggests that editing without recognition will not work. This recognition and subsequent revision can, of course, be facilitated by at least some instruction in grammar, whether it be formal or informal. At the same time, however, we should avoid the other extreme—the obsessive focus on error hunting. The drawbacks of the latter to writer esteem and, ultimately, to writing improvement are so obvious that they need no further comment. What is needed are not extreme positions but rather a middle ground where students can learn about the detection, consequences, and elimination of unconventional features without diminishing the desire to write and improve.

Undoubtedly, the failure of grammar instruction in the area of style has had strong repercussions in the overall evaluation of grammar instruction. The thinking goes, if grammar cannot help in style, an area where, by nature, it is most suited to help, then where can it help? If formal grammar instruction cannot help, at least directly help, in content and organization, then grammar instruction becomes, at best, solely an activity to raise students' scores on standardized grammar tests and, at worst, a way to keep students busy under the guise of "language improvement." Thus the stage is set to claim that the teaching of grammar should be abolished from the curriculum because it has no vital connection to writing and, hence, brings no benefit to writing. In short, a failure in one crucial part works to condemn the whole even more.

Making Grammar Instruction More Productive

Does grammar really belong in the school curriculum? Yes, I believe it does. Although it is possible to argue for inclusion on the grounds that the study of grammar teaches important analytic skills, that it offers a valuable means of learning about the nature of language, and that it constitutes a worthwhile intellectual activity in itself, I believe that the study of grammar can play a more productive role in writing improvement—but only with certain important modifications, as will become apparent in this study, particularly in Chapter 5. For the present, I tend to agree with the majority of past studies that indicate that formal grammar instruction, as commonly conceived and prac-ticed, has failed to produce significant writing improvement. This failure has resulted not so much because of a lack of effort on the part of teachers—many have spent their professional careers trying to bring fruitful results—but, ultimately, because expectations of gram-mar were unrealistic. Like the near-mythical omnipotence of cod-liver oil, the study of grammar became imbued with medicinal powers it simply did not possess, particularly with respect to writing ills. Given the present manner and substance of grammar instruction, the reach simply exceeded the grasp. This admission, however, is not meant to be a blanket condemnation of grammar instruction. As suggested in this chapter, areas exist where grammar and writing overlap and, hence, where grammar can bring potential benefits to writing. In these overlapping areas, however, grammar instruction has suffered from misguided aims, poor focus, and faulty methods. Thus, even in those areas where grammar can most directly make an impact on writing quality, it has often failed to do so. Conceiving and presenting grammar in the wrong way, we have not made grammar connect in the right way, neither to writing nor to students themselves, thereby leaving much of the potential of grammar untapped.

How can we more effectively tap this potential? Paradoxically, maximizing the benefits of grammar instruction to writing requires teaching less, not more, grammar. This means making grammar instruction both less expansive and more cost-efficient, which, in turn, should create more time for other kinds of writing instruction. If grammar instruction is to make a more productive contribution to writing improvement, we need to put into practice Hillocks's advice of approaching stylistic problems only "after careful task analysis and with minimal grammar" (1986, 248–49). We can begin making less grammar better by first directing and, more important, sharpening our focus on areas where grammar instruction ought to make a difference. These areas will constitute the chief concern of Chapter 2.

2 The Basics of a Writer's Grammar

In a time when the public perceives a drastic decline in writing skills, teachers face growing pressure to teach what is often called "basic grammar"—the traditional eight parts of speech, the major syntactic constructions and their functions, and a heavy dose of correct usage. Yet, in many ways, implementing the prescribed cure seems more problematic than the alleged disease. As any teacher can attest, teaching all the technical aspects of the so-called "basics" of grammar represents a formidable and time-consuming task. Worse yet, even if this task is accomplished, not all of these basics have relevance to the teaching of writing. Indeed, when many other aspects of writing require attention, teachers cannot simply saturate students with all the "basics" of grammar in hopes of covering just the ones relevant to writing. In order to make grammar connect more efficiently and more fruitfully to writing, teachers need to be more selective in what they teach. This means that we, as teachers, need to identify the real basics, the nitty-gritty of basic grammar, and, then, make these basics accessible to students as quickly and easily as possible.

At the outset, I wish to make clear the distinction between the teaching of grammar as an academic subject and the teaching of grammar as a tool for writing improvement. Although they may overlap to some extent, the two types of grammar instruction serve different purposes and, thus, have different goals. Grammar as an academic subject seeks to render as full and revealing a picture as possible of the systematic nature of language, particularly, the syntactic aspects of language. By so doing, it hopes to show not only the complexities of the language but also the various ways of analyzing those complexities. This type of grammar study is a self-contained, detailed, rigorous, and worthy intellectual endeavor in its own right. In contrast, grammar as a tool for writing is more limited in its scope and aims. Rather than seeking the fuller picture, this type of grammar study focuses on only those aspects of grammar that have relevance to writing. Thus the grammar taught is more selective and, in the end, much more basic. Because of its specific aim, this type of grammar should not be taught for its own sake (like grammar as an academic subject), nor should it be taught in isolation from writing activities. Ideally, this grammar will be integrated with writing instruction and presented as quickly as possible so that students can use it during the revision or proofreading stages of writing. In writing-centered programs, the general pedagogical aim should be not just to relate grammar instruction better to writing instruction but also to decrease grammar instruction so that more time can be devoted to all problems of writing, not just those pertaining to grammar. This diminution of grammar instruction does not, of course, mean that the excluded aspects of grammar are unworthy of study. They are, but they should be brought in only if they have a bearing on writing improvement.

Identifying the Basic Categories

Assuming that grammar can make some contribution to writing, how do we go about finding the real "basics" of grammar as they pertain to writing? These basics certainly cannot be all the grammatical categories teachers normally present since writing not only represents quite a different activity from grammatical analysis but also serves a different purpose. Within all the basic categories of formal grammar taught, what are the *really* basic ones, that is, the minimal set of categories most relevant to both grammar and writing? In other words, what grammatical categories represent the most economical yet utilitarian ones to teach for the purposes of improving writing? I believe these questions are of the utmost importance if teachers wish to relate better what they teach in grammar to what students produce in writing.

The traditional components of writing suggest where to begin the search. If skilled writing requires a mastery of content, organization, and style, and if formal grammar instruction has, as commonly believed, the most to offer in the area of style (defined broadly here), then we should consider as candidates at least those grammatical categories which most effectively aid in the improvement of style. Yet even here selectivity is needed, since students can and do make a wide variety of stylistic errors, ranging from syntactic (e.g., sentence fragments, nonparallel structure) and morphological errors (e.g., tense and number agreement errors) to semantic and pragmatic errors (e.g., diction errors, wrong tone) to graphological errors (e.g., faulty punctuation, misspelling). Grammar instruction obviously cannot remedy all these kinds of errors. A knowledge of grammatical categories cannot provide much help in reducing, for example, spelling errors or semantic/pragmatic errors since correction of these types of errors has little or no involvement with grammatical categories traditionally taught in the classroom. (Yet, note how many people clamor for more basic grammar instruction on the basis of such errors.) If we keep in mind what grammar can and cannot do, better prospects seem to lie with syntactic, morphological, and some graphological errors (e.g., faulty punctuation) since the treatment of these types of stylistic errors often involves grammatical categories. If so, then we should look more carefully within this more confined area in order to isolate the minimal set of grammatical categories.

Even within the more confined area, however, we still confront a wide diversity of error and, thus, a potentially large number of categories to teach. As teachers can attest, students make many kinds of syntactic, morphological, and punctuation errors. How, therefore, can we possibly limit even here the number of grammatical categories to teach? We can begin by concentrating on those categories which have the most pedagogical utility. Given the diverse kinds of stylistic errors that students make and the dearth of classroom time to address them, it makes little sense to focus on grammatical categories involved in correcting errors of low frequency. (I am here, of course, speaking of priorities and degrees, not absolutes.) Grammatical categories with narrow application may, indeed, be relevant and even helpful in correcting some isolated and infrequent errors, but the time needed to introduce the categories is usually not cost-efficient. On the other hand, it does seem to make a great deal of sense to focus on categories involved in correcting errors of high frequency. To give an obvious example, it makes considerably more sense to teach the concept "subject" than the concept "objective complement," since students more frequently make errors involving subjects (e.g., errors in subject-verb agreement) than those involving objective complements. By the same reasoning, it makes more sense to give priority to the category "verb" than to, say, the category "article," since verb errors occur more frequently than article errors (at least with native English writers). We can turn to some recent research in order to get a good picture of the kinds of stylistic errors that students make and their frequency.

The Connors-Lunsford Study

Through a comprehensive study of 3,000 graded college essays collected from teachers across the United States, Robert J. Connors and Andrea A. Lunsford (1988) were able to rank the most frequently

Table 1*

Error or error pattern (ranked by percent of total errors)	Percent of total errors (%)	Percent marked by teacher (%)	Rank by number of errors marked by teacher
1. No comma after introductory element	11.5	30	2
2. Vague pronoun reference	9.8	32	4
3. No comma in compound sentence	8.6	29	7
4. Wrong word	7.8	50	1
5. No comma in nonrestrictive element	6.5	31	10
6. Wrong/missing inflected endings	5.9	51	5
7. Wrong or missing preposition	5.5	43	8
8. Comma splice	5.5	54	6
9. Possessive apostrophe error	5.1	62	3
10. Tense shift	5.1	33	12
11. Unnecessary shift in person	4.7	30	14
12. Sentence fragment	4.2	55	9
13. Wrong tense or verb form	3.3	49	13
14. Subject-verb agreement	3.2	58	11
15. Lack of comma in series	2.7	24	19
16. Pronoun agreement error	2.6	48	15
17. Unnecessary comma with restrictive element	2.4	34	17
18. Run-on or fused sentence	2.4	45	16
19. Dangling or misplaced modifier	2.0	29	20
20. Its/it's error	1.0	64	18

*This table is a condensation of Table 1 from Connors and Lunsford (1988).

occurring "formal and mechanical" (i.e., stylistic) errors. Though their ranking derives from samples of college writing, I believe that the types of errors made have relevance to all teachers of writing. I reproduce in Table 1 two sets of frequency rankings given in the Connors-Lunsford study, one based on the percentage of total errors found in the graded essays and the other based on the percentage of errors actually marked by the original teacher. (Connors and Lunsford exclude from the rankings spelling errors, which, incidentally, ranked first.)

As might be expected from a nationwide sample, the twenty most frequent formal errors found in the Connors-Lunsford study comprise a variety of errors. These errors involve punctuation, for example, commas (1, 3, 5, 8, 15, 17) and apostrophes (9, 20); verbs (6, 10, 13, 14); pronouns (2, 11, 16); prepositions (7); diction (4); modifiers (19); and sentence boundaries (12, 18). Although the range of stylistic errors again suggests that isolating some basic categories on which to focus might prove difficult, if not impossible, certain clusters of errors seem to emerge within this diversity. For instance, five out of the top ten errors in terms of frequency of occurrence involve punctuation errors, either with apostrophes or, particularly, with commas. Indeed, going by the results of the Connors-Lunsford study, comma errors (1, 3, 5) make up three of the ten most frequently occurring stylistic errors, and the count rises to four out of ten if comma splices (8) are viewed as comma errors rather than as sentence boundary errors. Alternatively viewed, the number of errors related directly or indirectly to sentence or clause boundaries is strikingly high. Comma splices can be grouped here, as can sentence fragments (12) and run-on or fused sentences (18). We can also add to this group tense shift (10) and subject-verb agreement (14), both of which more indirectly yet crucially involve clause boundaries, the former requiring consistency of verb tense in main (not necessarily subordinate) clauses and the latter requiring consistency of number between subject and verb in the same clause (but not different clauses). Significantly, three out of six comma errors involve clause or sentence boundaries. The comma splice (8) has already been mentioned, but we can include in the sentence/clause boundary group the lack of commas in a compound sentence (3), which involves placing commas between independent clauses, and, the most frequent error of all, lack of a comma after an introductory element (1), which involves a comma fault at the onset of the main clause. All told, sentence or clause boundary errors constitute seven out of the top twenty stylistic errors and four out of the top ten stylistic errors in the Connors-Lunsford study. These numbers are not exceeded, as far as can be discerned, by any other grouping using traditional grammatical categories. If so, the high percentage of errors involving sentence or clause boundaries suggests that students wishing to avoid an assortment of frequently occurring stylistic errors would do well to have a solid working knowledge of what constitutes a sentence or a main clause. All this further suggests that the category "sentence" (or "independent clause") is one of the basic concepts, if not *the* basic concept, in not only grammar instruction but, more significantly, in remedying an assortment of stylistic errors.

Also of interest in the Connors-Lunsford study, as the two researchers duly note, are the differences between the rank based on frequency of occurrence (i.e., percentage of total error found in the graded essays) and the rank based on the actual marking of errors by the original teacher. For example, possessive apostrophe errors rank ninth on the basis of frequency of occurrence but third on the basis of marking by the teacher; diction errors rank fourth on the basis of frequency but first on the basis of marking by the teacher. Such findings confirm that, though errors often occur in papers, teachers do not always mark them (even when they are of the same kind). Further, the Connors-Lunsford data indicate that some errors are much more frequently marked by teachers than others. For example, 62 percent of the apostrophe errors were marked but only 29 percent of the dangling or misplaced modifiers. Connors and Lunsford speculate that this variability results from such factors as degree of seriousness or annoyance of the error to teacher or student, quickness or ease of marking, and perceived needs of the student. Thus, according to the authors, apostrophe errors are marked more often than sentence fragments, comma splices, and wrong verb tenses not because apostrophe errors are considered more serious but simply because they are easier to indicate as errors in essays. On the basis of their collected data, Connors and Lunsford find that college English teachers mark considerably fewer errors than is popularly believed. Of the most serious errors, for example, they mark on the average only 43 percent of those actually occurring. Further, they find that even among the most frequently marked errors, only two-thirds of those that occur are marked.

Even more on the positive side (at least, for grammar-loathing students and teachers) is that many stylistic errors in the top-twenty ranking can be treated without recourse to formal grammar. If this is so, we need not identify nor, more important, introduce in the classroom any grammatical categories associated with them. I mention here in passing spelling errors, even though Connors and Lunsford chose not to include them in their ranking. (As indicated earlier, had spelling errors been included, they would have ranked first in frequency.) Certainly, misspellings are treatable without the aid of formal grammar. Although misspellings occur within a host of grammatical categories (e.g., noun, verb, adjective), students do not need to be taught these categories in order to correct the misspellings. Of those stylistic errors that actually appear in the top-twenty ranking, a sizable number of them can also be handled without reliance on formal grammar. These include possessive apostrophe errors (9) and the possessive-versus-contraction *its/it's* error (20), which, despite the grammatical terminology, are essentially spelling errors, or at least, can be handled as such. (These errors occur only in writing—the distinctions are not relevant in speech.) Errors in diction (4), errors with prepositions (7), and most, if not all, of the errors involving reference of some sort (2, 11, 16, 19) can also be handled without bringing in formal grammatical categories. For example, to help students correct a word having vague pronoun reference (2), teachers can point out the word and ask what it refers to (or, on occasion, describes); the same kind of question can be asked in the case of dangling and misplaced modifiers (19); that is, teachers can ask, "What does this describe?" In brief, because some of the most frequently occurring errors found in the Connors-Lunsford study do not require a formal knowledge of grammar, we can, by either default or by selection, further decrease the number of grammatical categories to teach. Indeed, of the errors in the top-twenty ranking, we could, at minimum, eliminate eight of them (possessive apostrophe error, *its/it's* error, wrong word, wrong or missing preposition, vague pronoun reference, unnecessary shift in person, pronoun agreement error, dangling or misplaced modifier) as being better handled by an approach other than formal grammar.

As helpful as the Connors-Lunsford study may be, we should not view frequency as the sole or even most important factor in determining the minimal set of grammatical categories. While the frequency figures provided by Connors and Lunsford prove useful insofar as they reveal how often certain kinds of errors actually occur, the figures do not reveal (nor were they meant to reveal) the varying degrees of seriousness of the errors. Stated in another way, the most frequent errors may not necessarily be the most serious errors. Misspellings, for example, constitute the most frequent of all writing errors, but, for most teachers, they are not the most serious ones. Some difficulties intrude here since what is or is not a serious stylistic error often seems to lie in the eyes of the beholder. Some readers see certain stylistic errors as serious while others do not. Teachers (who certainly serve as readers) are not exempt from this variance. As Connors and Lunsford note, teachers often show this variance when they mark and, therefore, highlight certain types of stylistic errors while ignoring other types. It is important to keep in mind here that teachers' sensitivities to various stylistic errors can differ drastically from the public's. Indeed, that a comparatively high percentage of errors is left unmarked by teachers does not mean that they go unnoticed by teachers—or by others in positions that affect people's lives.

The Hairston Study

Maxine Hairston's (1981) attitudinal survey on common writing errors provides a clearer picture of what people in the professions consider "serious" errors. Hairston prepared a questionnaire which consists of sixty-five sentences, each containing a different error in standard usage, and which asks readers to indicate their reaction to each error (either "Does not bother me," "Bothers me a little," or "Bothers me a lot"). The questionnaire ends with the open-ended question, "What is the most annoying feature of the writing that comes across your desk?" The questionnaire was sent to 101 professional people (three-fourths were over forty), of whom 84 responded, 52 with written comments. The respondents, according to Hairston, represent 63 occupations other than English teaching (e.g., those of business executive, attorney, state legislator, computer program designer, architect, travel agency owner, county commissioner, bank president, newspaper columnist, realtor, oil company president, stock broker, federal judge, state educational commissioner). The results of the Hairston study indicate that the professionals surveyed, many of whom occupy high management positions in their fields, are highly aware of and often react strongly to certain kinds of formal and usage errors. Using the degree of reader reaction as a gauge, Hairston classified the errors into groups, from the most serious to the least serious, and provided typical examples. This classification appears in Figure 1.

Two points need to be stressed here. First, it is worth repeating that the errors above are classified according to the respondents' perceptions of the seriousness of the error. For example, the respondents generally reacted most strongly to "status-marking" errors (errors indicating the writer's social status, such as the use of *brung* rather than *brought, has went* rather than *has gone*, use of double negatives, use of objective-case pronouns as subjects). Status-marking errors tend to occur with speakers of nonstandard varieties of English, both non-

Status Marking

nonstandard verb forms in past or past participle: *brung* instead of *brought*; *had went* instead of *had gone*

lack of subject-verb agreement: *We was* instead of *We were*; *Jones don't think it's acceptable* instead of *Jones doesn't think it's acceptable*

double negatives

objective pronoun as subject: *Him and Richard were the last ones hired.*

Very Serious

sentence fragments

run-on sentences

noncapitalization of proper nouns

would of instead of *would have*

lack of subject-verb agreement (non–status marking)

insertion of comma between the verb and its complement

nonparallelism

faulty adverb forms: *He treats his men bad.*

use of transitive verb *set* for intransitive *sit*

Serious

predication errors: *The policy intimidates hiring.*

dangling modifiers

I as an objective pronoun

lack of commas to set off interrupters like *however*

lack of commas in a series

tense switching

use of a plural modifier with a singular noun: *These kind of errors*

Moderately Serious

lack of possessive form before a gerund

lack of commas to set off an appositive

inappropriate use of quotation marks

lack of subjunctive mood

writing *That is her across the street*

use of *whoever* instead of *whomever*

use of the construction *The situation is . . . when*

failure to distinguish between *among* and *between*

comma splices

Minor or Unimportant

use of a qualifier before *unique*: *That is the most unique city*

writing *different than* instead of *different from*

use of a singular verb with *data*

use of a colon after a linking verb: *Three causes of inflation are*:

omission of the apostrophe in the contraction *it's*

Figure 1. Hairston's error classification.

white and white. Just below the status-marking errors, the respondents showed strong reactions against a group of "very serious"
mechanical errors. These errors include sentence fragments, run-on
sentences, failure to capitalize proper nouns, use of *would of* instead of
would have, lack of subject-verb agreement, insertion of a comma
between verb and complement, lack of parallel structure, faulty
adverb form ("He treats his men bad"), and use of the transitive *set* for
intransitive *sit.* (As a group, most of these nonstandard features seem
to involve conventions peculiar to writing, particularly, formal writing; they also seem to occur in varying degrees in most, if not all,
varieties of English, both standard and nonstandard, white and
nonwhite.) A second point worth stressing is that, from Hairston's
study, we see that professionals other than teachers have a wide
variance of reaction to nonstandard stylistic features. Some nonstandard features apparently bothered people very much, while others
bothered them only moderately or hardly at all. Interestingly, of those
that elicited weak negative reactions (the "moderately serious" and
"minor or unimportant" groups), the majority involve either graphological conventions (e.g., punctuation) or semantic (rather than
syntactic) distinctions (e.g., *among* vs. *between, data* vs. *datum, its* vs. *it's,
different from* vs. *different than, unique* vs. *very unique)*. For the surveyed
professionals, the latter features, in varying degrees, fall into what
Mina Shaughnessy in *Errors and Expectations* would call "a territory of
tolerable error" (1977, 122). Of those features that elicited strong
negative reactions (the "status marking" and "very serious" groups),
many involve syntactic (rather than semantic) distinctions. These
differences will later take on importance in determining the minimal
set of categories for a writer's grammar.

For the present, however, it is important to realize that, while some
nonstandard stylistic features arouse only weak reactions, others
evoke strong negative reactions, specifically, from people in the
professions. It is also important to realize that, while such people do
not represent the only audience of writers, they probably represent
the most influential outside the classroom. Giving heed to this general
fact, Hairston concludes her study thus:

> I was not surprised to have the comments indicate that the
> qualities in writing that business and professional people value
> most are clarity and economy. I was surprised, however, at how
> vehement and specific they were about misspellings, faulty
> punctuation, and what they unabashedly call "errors." I think it is
> important for us and for our students to realize that this fairly
> representative sample of middle-aged and influential Americans
> has strong conservative views about usage. Although there seem

> to be some signs of change, and on some usage items the public
> may be ahead of the professions, I think that we cannot afford to
> let students leave our classrooms thinking that surface features of
> discourse do not matter. They do. (799)

I believe Hairston's conclusion deserves some comment, if only because the social consequences of "surface features" are sometimes given short shrift or ignored completely in pro-grammar versus anti-grammar debates. Some may with good reason object that Hairston's findings are not representative because of the makeup of her population sample. Hairston admits that her sample does not cover all professions and that it is slanted more towards middle-aged male Texans. Yet her study may err more on the side of moderation than actual neglect. Although not every profession was surveyed and although not all professionals in the United States are Texans, Hairston's respondents do seem to represent at least three salient characteristics of professionals. First, because of socioeducational and experience requirements for entry and advancement into the middle and upper levels of the professions, most tend to be middle-aged; second, because of past—and still present—sociocultural barriers confronting women, the majority of professionals also tend to be male; last, because of the generally high status accorded to the professions, many professionals occupy positions of influence (a fact certainly brought out by perusing Hairston's examples of respondents to the survey). The age and gender biases here interact with the degree of influence and, ultimately, I believe, with the degree of negative reactions toward the nonstandard stylistic features.

Consider first the factor of age. It is commonly believed that younger people tend to be more tolerant of differences, including language differences, than older people. Put in another way, we tend to think of older people as more conservative in their views toward language differences and language change than their younger counterparts. If this is so, it has a bearing on the kinds of reactions elicited by the nonstandard stylistic features. If the professionals in Hairston's sample were younger, they would probably be more tolerant of the nonstandard features, but these younger respondents, because of their age, would also be less likely to occupy the higher positions of influence or power in their profession. If the respondents were older, they would be more likely to occupy positions of influence or power, and, at the same time, also probably be more conservative in their views toward language differences and change (and, hence, more apt to have negative reactions to the nonstandard features tested in Hairston's study).

The gender bias in the sample also tends to temper the degree of negative reactions found in the study. Indeed, if Hairston's sample included more female respondents, the degree of negative reactions for many of the nonstandard items tested would have, in all likelihood, increased rather than decreased. Many studies indicate that females are generally more sensitive to, and thus generally employ, standard or more prestigious forms in language. For example, Fischer (1958) found that girls as early as three to ten years of age use the more prestigious *-ing* present participle ending on verbs much more frequently than do boys of a comparable age, who use the less prestigious *-in'* ending. Levine and Crockett (1966) found that white females (along with those of higher education and those in prestigious occupations) pronounced postvocalic /r/ (the more prestigious variant, as opposed to the deletion of postvocalic /r/) more frequently than white males; Trudgill (1972), in a study conducted in Norwich, England, found that women tend to use "standard" English more frequently than do men in order to compensate for their subordinate status. Shuy et al. (1967), in a study investigating Detroit speech, found that women showed greater sensitivity to standard forms than did men by their avoidance of such syntactic forms as multiple negation (e.g., *Nobody can't go*) and pronominal apposition (e.g., *My brother, he went to the park*). Finally, Labov (1972), in a study conducted in New York City, found that women in careful speech are less apt to use nonprestigious forms than are men, and that during linguistic change women serve as an innovative force when neutral forms are involved but as a conservative force when nonprestigious forms are involved. Adding more female professionals to Hairston's sample, then, would most likely lead to a higher, not lower, degree of negative reaction from the respondents. This resulting increase would not, of course, make the professional public's assessments of writing quality any more correct, but it would make them more representative of the general population.

Despite the skewing in the sample population, the reactions revealed in Hairston's study do seem to reflect those of many professionals throughout the United States. Rightly or wrongly, the professional public, whether male or female, can be offended, sometimes very strongly, by apparently minor features of writing. If anything, Hairston's concluding comments remind us, just as we constantly remind our students, that it pays to write with the audience in mind. Furthermore, while Hairston notes that the kinds of errors perceived as serious by the professional public may change in time, this change occurs slowly and unevenly. Historically, changes in language attitudes do take place, as exemplified by the fact that most educated people today no longer condemn or even perceive, say, the loss of distinction between *will* and *shall* or the lack of subjunctive mood in verbs. Yet changes in language attitudes, particularly deep-set and widespread ones, usually occur across several decades, sometimes across several generations, almost always too long a time for present writers to wait to appeal their cases. Studies by Shuy (1973) and Anderson (1981) attest to the tenacity of these language attitudes.

Lastly, Hairston's concluding comments should make us consider more carefully our role in handling the offending nonstandard features. Although it may be easy for teachers to dismiss these features as merely "superficial," the surface apparently has considerable importance to those who often hold the power to affect other people's lives. If Hairston's findings are accurate but we choose to ignore them, we may unnecessarily make our students' writing vulnerable to disparagement—and, sometimes, severe ridicule—by people whom upwardly mobile students presumably seek most to impress. In particular, we disproportionately put at risk students who speak a nonstandard variety of English since they are the ones most likely to reproduce in their writing the "status marking" and "very serious" errors so roundly condemned by the professionals. While we as teachers know (or should know) that nonstandard varieties of English are just as systematic as standard ones, an influential segment of the public does seem to judge certain salient dialectal and stylistic features as serious errors, so serious that these features apparently outweigh other and probably better indicators of writing quality. As writers themselves, teachers are well aware of this danger and thus take care to avoid such socially stigmatized features, even when their occupation remains undisclosed. If so, it seems inconsistent for us to ignore such features in student writing and to advise our students not to worry about "superficial errors" when we, in our own writings, do just the opposite. If the global aim of writing is, as Linda Flower (1979) suggests, to transform writer-based prose into reader-based prose and thereby create favorable impressions in readers, then we do better service to our students by disclosing the rhetorical and social consequences of such features, and, just as important, showing them ways to avoid these features in formal writing. Moreover, if it turns out that the adverse reactions to certain linguistic features ultimately result not from the features themselves but from the social groups that produce them, then it seems far more enlightening and productive to remove the linguistic features as a cover and to expose the prejudice for what it is. That is, if people in power unfairly make it difficult for certain social groups to climb the socioeconomic ladder, we should not give these perpetrators an opportunity to hide the more underlying causes by letting them use nonstandard features of writing as the discriminating factor.

In the end, it boils down to questions of practicality. If a rough analogy may be made, the problem of nonstandard or unconventional forms in formal writing is somewhat akin to wearing jeans and sneakers when the occasion calls for a suit and dress shoes. It is not that jeans and sneakers are intrinsically wrong and that a suit and dress shoes are intrinsically right. (Who, in their right mind, would wear the latter attire to an outing at the beach?) Rather, different situations call for different styles. The choice of style (or dialect, as the case may be) is no less significant in language, particularly in writing, where the nature of the medium heightens the assumption that addressers have taken the time to refine their message to meet the needs and expectations of the addressees. Yet, if students know very little of the kinds of stylistic options available and even less of the consequences of their choice, then what they do not know may, indeed, hurt them in the end. Ignorance may be bliss, but not forever.

The dilemma that inevitably confronts us is, do we as teachers try to change the professional public's overweighted and often shortsighted allegiance to its conception of acceptable style, or do we give more attention to certain features of style during the revision and proofreading stages of the writing process so that our students can circumvent the negative responses? If history offers any lessons here, the first alternative of changing the perceptions of the professional public, assuming it can be achieved, will come about through evolution, not revolution. To think otherwise risks making too many of our present students into sacrificial lambs. In an ideal world, all writers would know exactly how readers will perceive their writing, and all readers would know how to judge writing quality fairly. Unfortunately, and to repeat an old cliché, it is not an ideal world, and, given the depth of feeling aroused by certain kinds of unconventional features, teachers stand a better chance of changing the writing habits of students than of changing the seemingly knee-jerk reactions of offended readers.

A Comparison of the Findings

Matching the findings of Hairston's attitudinal survey with the frequency ranking of Connors and Lunsford helps limit still further the kinds of stylistic errors, and hence grammatical categories, that teachers can profitably focus on in the classroom. To conflate two key ideas brought out earlier, it makes little practical sense to teach grammatical categories in isolation from the kinds of stylistic errors that students actually make and from the kinds of reactions the errors evoke. If this is so, teachers should not be overly concerned if errors producing weak negative reactions occur with relatively high frequency or if errors producing strong negative reactions occur with relatively low frequency. Such errors have lower priority and can be handled in time. A real cause for concern, however, would be the worst-case scenario, where errors producing strong negative reactions occur with high frequency. It is enlightening to compare here the findings of the Hairston study with those of the Connors-Lunsford study. On the good side, many of the errors which fall in either the "status marking" or "very serious" group (e.g., double negatives, objective pronoun as subject, nonparallelism, comma between subject and complement) do not turn up at all in the Connors-Lunsford "top twenty," and, conversely, many of the items in the top twenty do not turn up in Hairston's "status marking" or "very serious" groups. The bad part is that some do. With the "status marking" errors, the worst-case scenario occurs with wrong verb forms (e.g., *brung* instead of *brought*, *set* instead of *sit*); with the "very serious" errors, we have sentence fragments, run-on sentences, and subject-verb agreement errors. These errors should be given high priority, particularly—and preferably—during the revising and proofreading stages of the writing process.

After having started from a seeming morass of stylistic errors and a seemingly equal morass of grammatical categories, we now arrive at, I hope, a better picture of just which ones need the most attention. It appears that certain stylistic errors, because of their relatively high frequency of occurrence *and* because of the high degree of stigma attached to them, will present special problems for students both in and, perhaps particularly, out of the classroom. If such features of writing will produce negative public evaluations—despite the overall quality of the writing—teachers have a responsibility not only to inform students of the possible socioeconomic penalties but also to provide means to detect and eliminate these features. Having isolated the more serious errors from the diverse kinds that students make, we now also get a clearer picture of the grammatical categories on which to focus (or at minimum, which ones to avoid). Given the frequency and the social consequences of certain kinds of stylistic errors and given our initial constraints of generality and utility, it makes little sense from a practical standpoint to deem as "basic" such syntactic constructions as nominative absolutes, infinitive phrases, noun adjuncts, phrasal verbs, and the like, or even such grammatical functions as direct and indirect objects. Nor does it make much sense to label as basic all the traditional eight parts of speech, since not all of them are relevant in correcting the most serious kinds of errors. Though writers certainly write with such elements, there seems no great need to identify and refer to them specifically by name, particularly when no highly frequent stigmatized feature is associated with them.

As suggested earlier, in determining the really basic categories on which to focus, it is important to separate syntactic (or structural) errors from usage errors (and, ultimately, syntactic categories from semantic ones). Although the distinction between syntactic errors and usage errors sometimes becomes blurred, usage errors are viewed primarily as vocabulary or diction errors, or to state it somewhat simplistically, usage errors involve the wrong choice of word, not the wrong choice of syntactic structure or relation. Thus, the choice of *brung* rather than *brought*, or *set* rather than *sit* constitutes a usage error. In contrast, sentence fragments and errors in subject-verb agreement are syntactic errors because they involve relationships between words (i.e., syntactic structure). The distinction between usage errors and syntactic errors is important for pedagogical reasons since the former, being essentially nonsyntactic in nature, can more easily be treated without formal grammar. In the treatment of *brung* vs. *brought*, for example, students do not need to learn formally such concepts as "past tense," "past participle," or even "verb." All they need to know is which standard forms substitute for the nonstandard forms and when such substitutions should be made (e.g., in formal writing). Significantly, and perhaps fortunately, most of Hairston's "status-marking" errors (e.g., *brung* vs. *brought*) are usage errors and thus can be handled without recourse to grammatical categories. However, a majority of the errors that Hairston lists as "very serious" (sentence fragments, run-on sentences, lack of subject-verb agreement, nonparallelism) are syntactic errors. For these errors, a knowledge of some formal grammatical categories may prove useful since the remedy is not a matter of mere substitution.

To recapitulate, grammar should be made into a more efficient and useful resource for writing improvement. This potential, however, has never been fully realized because grammar instruction has lacked a proper focus. Much, probably too much, grammar has been taught without taking into account the kinds and quantity of errors students actually make in writing. To bring in a contemporary metaphor, grammar teachers have engaged more in saturation bombing rather than in surgical strikes. Although students make many kinds of errors in writing (e.g., errors in content, organization, and style), grammar, as it is presently conceived and practiced, can aid most in remediating errors pertaining to style. Within the area of style, students make many kinds of errors, ranging from sentence fragments to errors in pronoun reference to errors in diction to errors in spelling and punctuation. Some of these errors (e.g., errors in spelling), because they are primarily graphological in nature, can be handled without reference to formal grammar; others (e.g., errors in pronoun reference and diction), because they are more semantic than syntactic in nature, can probably be handled better by meaning approaches than by formal grammar; the remainder, because they require some minimal knowledge of syntactic categories, can be handled with at least some recourse to formal grammar. Not all these errors, however, need to be given the same emphasis. Some of the errors occur infrequently; some, even if they do occur, are not especially noticed, or if they are, do not carry any great social penalties. Uncovering the minimal set of categories to teach, that is, the basics of basic grammar, then, requires attention to various factors, including the general utility of the category, the nature of the overlap between grammar and writing, and the relationship between the frequency and the social consequences of errors.

A Minimal Set of Categories

Given the foregoing, what precisely constitutes the minimal set of categories to present in the classroom? I suggest that teachers, particularly in the language arts, start—and, for minimalists, perhaps, even end—with the following: sentence (or independent clause), subject, verb, and modifier. Although these four units may at first seem woefully inadequate to hard-working grammar teachers, I present this "bare bones" set because of their potential utility in identifying and correcting the more frequent and more highly stigmatized stylistic errors. At the very least, students will need some idea of what constitutes a sentence (in contrast to a nonsentence) in order to correct sentence boundary errors (fragments and run-ons); they will need a notion of what constitutes a subject and a verb, not necessarily to identify sentences or independent clauses (although that will help), but in order to identify and correct subject-verb agreement errors (and other incorrect verb forms); last, they will need a general notion of what a modifier is to identify and correct various (not all) kinds of punctuation errors. While these categories are not applicable to all the major stylistic errors identified by the Connors-Lunsford and Hairston studies, they are applicable to a significant number of them.

Given the minimal set of categories above, we can group the categories in the following manner to show their relationship:

I. Sentence
II. Nonsentence
  A. Fragment
    1. Modifier
    2. Subject
    3. Verb

That is, a sentence and a nonsentence will be viewed as the two primary and contrasting categories. What is not a sentence is by definition a nonsentence. Further, what is a nonsentence is exemplified by, among other things, a fragment (only a part of a sentence, thus, a nonsentence). Modifiers, subjects, and verbs are examples of fragments; being fragments, they are also nonsentences. At this point, it is not necessary to further differentiate the six categories. A sentence does not, for example, have to be distinguished as either simple or complex, or modifiers as prepositional phrases or relative clauses or even as adjectives or adverbs. Again, the chief aim is not to teach all the basics of grammar but rather to focus on a minimal set of grammatical categories and to use these categories to treat a maximum number of the most serious stylistic errors. This more limited aim of grammar instruction should, as pointed out earlier, reduce the time devoted to formal grammar instruction and, hopefully, at the same time, make grammar connect better to writing.

The Utility of the Categories

What makes this minimal set of categories all the more useful is that the categories are applicable not only to many of the most serious kinds of stylistic errors but also to many of the less serious but highly frequent kinds of stylistic errors. Comma errors again prove a case in point. Though not classified as a serious kind of error in Hairston's study, comma errors, as noted earlier, account for four of the top ten most frequently occurring errors in the Connors-Lunsford study. (I include here comma splices as a comma error.) For example, in terms of frequency of occurrence, the lack of a comma after an introductory element ranks first. This "introductory element" lacking the comma is, of course, some sort of modifier. The present set of grammatical categories should facilitate correction here, since "modifier" constitutes one of the basic categories. The task is made simpler, however, in two ways. First, the category of modifiers is not, indeed, need not, be broken down into the various kinds of modifiers (e.g., prepositional phrase, adverbial clause, nominative absolute, participial phrase). If the category need not be broken down, teachers need not spend time teaching the various kinds of modifiers. Second, modifiers, for the purpose of correcting the comma error here, need only be defined as nonsentences or fragments. If so, rather than having several different kinds of comma rules involving an introductory modifier, teachers can work with a very general comma rule, namely, "If a fragment occurs before a sentence, it is set off from the sentence by a comma." While this rule will not solve all comma problems with introductory elements (for example, the question of the length of the modifier will have to be addressed), it does have the advantage of avoiding the introduction of new grammatical terminology, specifically, all the various types of introductory elements.

The three other common comma problems—lack of commas in compound sentences, lack of commas in nonrestrictive elements, and comma splices—are also potentially treatable with the minimal set of categories. The traditional comma rule about compound sentences (i.e., "A comma should set off independent clauses in a compound sentence") hinges crucially on identifying compound sentences, which first requires identifying independent clauses (i.e., sentences) within the larger sentence. Since the minimal set of categories contains all the relevant technical terms here (i.e., sentence or independent clause), no new technical terms need be introduced to identify compound sentences. Comma faults involving nonrestrictive elements are also treatable within the confines of the basic categories. Nonrestrictive elements, which in writing are set off by commas, have three general linguistic properties in common: (1) semantically, they add nonessential information within a sentence; (2) syntactically, they share various surface forms (e.g., relative clauses, participial phrases, prepositional phrases); and (3) syntactically, they usually follow immediately the person, place, or thing they modify or describe. Although formal grammar, as it is commonly taught in the schools, cannot easily incorporate the semantic property, teachers can help students to identify nonrestrictive elements by defining them as fragments which immediately follow the person, place, or thing they describe and which may be deleted without changing the essential meaning of the sentence. Again, no new grammatical terminology need be introduced. Last, the minimal set of categories can also be of use in correcting comma splices. Comma splices involve the incorrect joining of independent clauses by a comma alone (e.g., *Jack ate two hamburgers, Betty ate a ham sandwich.*) The crux of the problem here is identifying the independent clauses. As with the other four comma errors discussed above, the minimal set of categories proves relevant since it contains the category "sentence," or "independent clause," the crucial category in identifying comma splices.

Conclusion

Isolating the basic grammatical categories, then, offers several significant pedagogical advantages. For one, it obviates the need to teach grammar en masse, as has been the customary practice. With less material to present, teachers can more easily organize and present their lessons; with less material to absorb, students should retain more and be able to apply more readily what they have learned. Spending less time on grammar also means more time to spend on other, perhaps more pressing, matters of writing instruction (e.g., content and organization). The shortening of classroom hours devoted to grammar is not meant to imply that grammar instruction is irrelevant to writing improvement. Rather, it reemphasizes that grammar instruction can and should be made more cost-efficient than it is now. As an added bonus, less time devoted to grammar may help decrease the aversion that students typically develop towards the subject. If grammar is the proverbial worst subject of students, it comes as no surprise, given the complexity and abstractness of the subject and, unfortunately, the tediousness with which it has been taught. If limiting the number of grammatical categories offers anything of value, it at least means teaching less of what students loathe; more optimistically, it means a more opportune starting point to develop in students curiosity and, perhaps, even fascination.

Last, and equally important, isolating the basic grammatical categories makes clearer and, I believe, more achievable (at least, at one level) the linkage between grammar instruction and writing improvement. Yet, as suggested earlier, grammar, as it is presently conceived and taught, is not and cannot be a panacea for all writing ills. Although this study will later suggest how links can be made to the often-neglected areas of content and organization, the most direct link is to the area of style. If grammar instruction is properly focused in this area and properly presented, it can help students remedy a considerable number of frequently occurring and socially stigmatizing stylistic errors.

Isolating a minimal set of grammatical categories, then, has potential benefits. These benefits, however, remain only potential unless we find some effective way to present the minimal set of categories in the classroom. Do we still use the old-fashioned methods of rote memorization, oral drills, and written exercises? Or is there a better way? These questions become the chief concern of Chapter 3.

3 Teaching the Basics of a Writer's Grammar

At first sight, teaching only the grammatical categories relevant to the improvement of writing—for example, sentence, subject, verb, modifier—would not seem an overly difficult task. It would certainly be easier than teaching all the categories in a comprehensive grammar like Otto Jespersen's seven-volume *Modern English Grammar on Historical Principles* or even the categories from the more recent one-volume, 1,779-page *A Comprehensive Grammar of the English Language* by Randolph Quirk et al. Teaching a minimal set of grammatical categories would also seem easier than teaching what many teachers often present as "basic" grammar, that is, the traditional eight parts of speech, the major syntactic constructions and their functions, along with a heavy dose of correct usage. Yet, as these teachers can readily attest, presenting even a small number of grammatical categories, such as sentence, subject, verb, and modifier, can prove a difficult, time-consuming, not to mention frustrating, experience for both teachers and students. The problem stems from the methods teachers customarily use and, ultimately, from the nature of grammar and grammatical description. If we wish to give students a sounder working knowledge of a minimum number of grammatical categories and thereby make grammar a more efficient and effective tool for writing improvement, we need to present the grammatical categories in ways that are less time-consuming and more accessible to students.

The Problems of Teaching Grammatical Categories

The problems associated with teaching grammatical categories, even a small set of them, become readily apparent if we try to introduce even a basic category such as "sentence" (or, roughly, "independent clause"). The notion of sentence is important in writing if only because formal writing consists of an organized sequence of sentences. More particularly, the notion of sentence is also involved in correcting some frequent and highly resistant syntax-based stylistic errors, such as sentence fragments, run-ons, comma splices, and several kinds of errors involving punctuation, most notably commas and semicolons. Yet instilling students with a working knowledge of the category "sentence" usually proves an exasperating undertaking. Common sense might suggest that all we need to do here is to present students with a notional, or semantic, definition of a sentence, such as, "A sentence is any group of words which expresses a complete thought." To define a sentence in this way will not, unfortunately, always differentiate a sentence from a nonsentence. Consider the sequence *Jim didn't do his math homework. Because he hates it with a passion.* Certainly, *Jim didn't do his math homework* constitutes a complete thought and hence, by the given semantic definition, is a sentence. A student could, however, plausibly argue that *Because he hates it with a passion* also expresses a complete thought and hence is also a sentence. The same holds for sequences like *What a winner!* or *Good evening, Mr. Jones* or *Ah, to visit Paris in the spring.* Notice that simply questioning students about the lack of a "doer" in such sequences will not always produce the "complete thought." Indeed, for the sequence *Ah, to visit Paris in the spring,* asking for the doer might result in revisions like *Ah, for me to visit Paris in the spring* or *Ah, if I could visit Paris in the spring.* The main problem with defining a sentence semantically as "a complete thought," then, is specifying just what qualifies as a complete thought. Unfortunately, that often depends on the person with the thought. If the purveyor of the thought can reply, "It may not be a complete thought to you, but it's a complete thought to me," there is little, if anything, that teachers can do—at least from a semantic standpoint—to change the view. Chiding the person for having (or writing with) partial thoughts will not work either if we consider that partial thoughts, whatever they are, are still thoughts, and if these "partial" thoughts make sense to their producer, they are, for that person, complete. In short, while a complete thought and a sentence may overlap to a considerable degree, the areas of nonoverlap are large enough and problematic enough to make identification of sentences unreliable.

If defining a sentence semantically is unsatisfactory, we might resort to another commonly used definition, namely, "A sentence is a group of words having a complete subject and a complete predicate." Leaving aside the recurring problem of what is meant by "complete," we still confront the problem of defining what is meant by "subject" and "predicate." Consider first the seemingly easier of the two, the problem of defining "subject." Many teachers try to equate subject with doer; that is, a subject is the doer or actor of the action expressed in the sentence. In many cases, however, this will not work for the simple reason that sentences often do not express an action, and, hence, lack a doer (e.g., *The temperature is low today* or *Mike's two books lay on the table* or *My younger brother did absolutely nothing yesterday*). Worse yet, even if the sentence expresses an action, the subject of the sentence still may not be the doer of that action (e.g., *The door suddenly opened* or *It is a fact that American soldiers fought in World War II* or *Jogging is slow running*). If defining a subject is difficult, defining "predicate" proves even more so. We can try equating predicate with the verb and its modifiers, but that would involve the burdensome task of defining "verb" and "modifier." Still worse, we would mislead students, since predicates more often than not involve not just verbs and their possible modifiers but also verb complements (e.g., direct object, indirect object, predicate nominative, objective complement, and all their modifiers). In brief, in trying to define "predicate," we run the risk of opening up a can brimming with grammatical worms. Retreating but still undaunted, we might try another tack and define a sentence as "a string of words containing a noun-phrase subject and an associated verb phrase." This definition, being more syntactically based (and less semantically based) than the preceding definitions, would seem to offer students a more accessible working definition of a sentence. Unfortunately, it does not. Even if we were able to define "subject" and "associated" in a manner clear enough for students to understand, we still would face in this definition the formidable tasks of defining "noun" (and all its modifiers) and "verb" (and all its modifiers and complements and complement modifiers). As a last resort, we might try to define verb phrase (or predicate) negatively— all that which is not the (complete) subject (or subject noun phrase). However, this ploy only sends us back to the previous problem of defining the subject (or noun phrase), not to mention the problem of specifying the meaning of "complete." Thus what first looks like a simple task again ends up as an incredibly time-consuming and, inevitably, frustrating undertaking.

The Root of the Problem

The root of the definitional problem lies in the nature of grammatical description, and, ultimately, in the nature of language itself. All human languages (and their dialects) work in rule-governed ways, or put in another way, all human languages (and their dialects) are systematic. If they were not so, humans could not learn them so readily as children. The systematicity of English is probably most obvious in syntax, for example, in the regular way we sequence elements in declarative sentences (e.g., usually subject first, verb next, and, if necessary, complement following) or in the regular way we form commands and yes-no questions. This systematicity pervades not just the syntax of a language but all levels of language—phonological, semantic, pragmatic. Language has often and aptly been called a "system of subsystems." Grammars of a language, whether traditional, structural, or transformational/generative in approach, try to describe this system, not only of the parts but also of the whole. Grammatical description reflects this systematicity of language, as it must if it seeks an accurate description of the language. Thus, for example, smaller parts are often described in relationship to larger parts, or larger parts to smaller parts. This method of description, it should be noted, characterizes not just descriptions of language systems but descriptions of all systems (e.g., planetary system, political system, family system, digestive system, traffic-control system).

That languages are systematic and are described as such allows us to make an important distinction between two kinds of rules concerning language: rules *of* language (i.e., descriptive rules) and rules *about* language (i.e., prescriptive, or usage, rules). Rules *of* language (e.g., those of English) are rules which involve only the self-contained system. Violations of the descriptive rules of English result in "non-English." Take, for example, the descriptive rule "Articles (*a, an, the*) precede nouns." The sentence *The girl is tall,* with the article *the* preceding the noun *girl*, is English, but **Girl the is tall,*[1] which violates the descriptive rule of article and noun sequencing, is not English, even though it contains English words. In contrast to rules *of* language, rules *about* language (i.e., prescriptive, or usage, rules) involve language and an external social system which regulates the choice of linguistic variants. Violations of the prescriptive rules still result in English sentences, even though the sentences may not be socially approved. Consider the two prescriptive rules "Don't use the word *ain't*" and "Don't end a sentence with a preposition." The sequences *Sam ain't going* and *Whom did you give the gift to?* violate prescriptive rules, but they are English sentences as much as *Sam isn't going* and *To whom did you give the gift?*

That languages are systematic and are described as such means that the study of grammar is, to a large extent, self-contained. This means that interrelationships of elements make up a large, if not the most important, portion of grammar study. Stated in a slightly different way, parts of the language system (e.g., parts of speech, larger constructions, rules of formation) must necessarily be described—and defined—in relation to other parts. Thus, a sentence is sometimes defined as a group of words composed of a complete subject and a complete predicate or as a string of words composed of a noun-phrase subject and a verb phrase. The fact that English (like all other languages) is systematic makes it easier for grammarians to describe language since they can state regularities succinctly in terms of relationships among elements. (Think how difficult description would be if the elements of English sentences occurred randomly.) The fact that grammatical descriptions of English reflect the systematicity of language, however, makes it difficult for teachers to introduce important categories such as "sentence" or "subject," since categories are often defined in terms of other categories.

The Difficulty for Students

Given the nature and number of interlinking definitions, it is no wonder that teachers have experienced great difficulty in getting students to master formal grammar, even a selected small portion of it. It would be no exaggeration to claim that students trying to learn even a small portion of grammar resemble cryptographers trying to decipher Egyptian hieroglyphics. Both processes involve analyses of languages found in antiquity; one, the written language of ancient Egypt; the other, the metalanguage (i.e., a language used to describe language) of grammar originating in ancient Greece. Both involve interrelated linguistic entities; one, the actual words of a language; the other, a set of abstract grammatical categories. Both crucially involve the cracking of a code to understand the meaning of the language; one, of the writing code; the other, of an interlinking metalanguage. Where the decipherment of Egyptian hieroglyphics was aided greatly by the accidental discovery of the Rosetta stone in 1799, the decipherment of grammatical terminology has not, in the main, been aided by any comparable code-breaking information, including, and perhaps especially, information contained in most grammar textbooks.

Cracking the Grammar Code

How can students crack the "grammar code"? How can they gain a working knowledge of basic grammatical categories such as sentence, subject, verb, etc., if such categories are defined in terms of other categories? Isn't it much like looking up the word *structure* in a dictionary and finding the definition "form" and under the entry for *form* finding the definition "structure"? I believe students can crack the grammar code but not by the time-consuming and frustrating methods of the past. The solution lies not in presenting semantic or compositional definitions, which inevitably entail either opaque or interlinking definitions of the categories, but rather in operational definitions. By an operational definition here, I mean a definition which defines by means of what an entity does or can have done to it rather than what comprises the entity. To cite a mundane example outside of grammar, one definition of *water* would be an aqueous chemical compound composed of two atoms of hydrogen and one atom of oxygen. This definition focuses on the composition of the entity and thus resembles many of the problematic definitions found in the study of grammar (e.g., "A sentence is composed of a subject and a predicate"). In contrast, an operational definition of *water* would be a liquid ingested by plants and animals to sustain life, or, perhaps, a liquid used to wash and rinse cars, dishes, etc. Granted, operational definitions are not as impressive or as delimiting as nonoperational definitions. The important point here is that they do not have to be. All that is required of operational definitions is that they work in actual use and that they avoid interlinking technical terms, something which the nonoperational definition of *water* does not do.

The Underlying Knowledge of "Pronoun"

As startling as it may sound at first, all students who have acquired English as a native language (as well as many who have acquired it non-natively) already possess an immense knowledge of the operations (i.e., descriptive rules) of English, including its syntax. This must be so, or they would not be able to produce grammatical sentences in everyday conversation. This knowledge, however, is largely unconscious. Students normally cannot explain the operations, or rules, but the knowledge is nonetheless there and waiting to be tapped. Consider pronouns. Most grammar books state explicitly that a pronoun is a word that "substitutes for a noun." Yet this traditional definition of pronoun is clearly incorrect, or at least incomplete, since a pronoun can substitute not just for a noun (e.g., *boys → they*) but also, among other things, a noun phrase (e.g., *the noisy boys in the back of the room → they*) or any construction that functions as a noun or noun phrase, including other pronouns (e.g., *he and she → they*). Indeed, if students dutifully mastered and meticulously applied the grammar-book definition of a pronoun and only that, they would be unable to identify many pronoun substitutions in the language. Whether grammar books state the definition of a pronoun correctly or completely, fortunately, does not really matter in the end. Native students already unconsciously know the correct version of the pronoun substitution rule; otherwise they could not use pronouns in everyday conversation.

If given the following sentences and personal pronouns, students who are native speakers of English would find little difficulty in substituting the pronoun for the appropriate word or words in the sentence:

1. Jane and Bob bought a book during the trip to San Francisco. (*she*)

2. He and she live in New York City. (*they*)

3. It was the Beatles who first made British rock music popular. (*they* or *them*)

4. That Mary studied hard was very clear to John. (*it*)

5. Most people believe that the world is round. (*it*)

6. Sometimes, exercising can be relaxing. (*it*)

Items 1–6 above illustrate two important facts concerning personal pronouns. First, personal pronouns do, indeed, substitute for a variety of constructions in English. In (1), *she* substitutes for the noun *Jane*; in (2), *they*, for the compound pronoun *he and she*; in (3), *they*, for the noun phrase *the Beatles*; in (4), *it*, for the noun clause *that Mary studied hard*; in (5), *it*, for the noun clause *that the world is round* or, alternatively, for the noun phrase *the world*; in (6), *it*, for the gerund *exercising*. Second, errors involving prescriptive rules (i.e., usage errors) may often occur but errors involving descriptive rules rarely occur. For example, in (3), students may substitute the pronoun *them* for *the Beatles* instead of the more formal *they*. However, this is a very different type of error from substituting a personal pronoun for *made* (a verb) or for *popular* (an adjective). Stated more generally, though students may substitute the incorrect form of a personal pronoun, they will never substitute a personal pronoun for any grammatical category other than a noun, a noun phrase, or a construction that serves as such.

The above exercise with personal pronouns helps point out some significant advantages of operational definitions in the teaching of grammar. If students can substitute pronouns for the appropriate word or words in exercises like (1–6) above and in utterances of daily speech—in ignorance of or, perhaps, despite the inaccuracy or incompleteness of the common textbook definition—then teachers do not really have to teach the definition of pronoun, not even the operational one. Students already have that knowledge. Put in a more general way, teachers cannot teach students what they already know. Although students probably cannot state the operation of pronoun substitution in the metalanguage of grammar, they must already possess the tacit knowledge that a personal pronoun, at the least, is a word that can take the place of a noun, noun phrase, or something that functions as either. (The foregoing is a rough operational definition of a personal pronoun.) Again, without this kind of unconscious linguistic knowledge, students would be unable to make pronoun substitutions for the appropriate words in daily speech.

The fact that students already have such knowledge can also help teachers clarify some facts about English grammar. If students already unconsciously know that a personal pronoun can substitute for a noun, noun phrase, or some construction that functions as either, then they must also know that these elements which accept pronoun substitution are all syntactically (though not necessarily semantically) similar. That is, despite the various forms and lengths which these units take, students already unconsciously know that they function as one category, namely, that of noun. Indeed, precisely because the noun clauses *that Mary studied hard* and *that the world is round* in (4) and (5) above allow the personal pronoun *it* as a proper substitution, teachers can plausibly argue that these constructions, while not having the form of nouns, are functioning as nouns. That is, even though the shapes are different, the function is the same. This fact is important since it means teachers can use pronoun substitution as an operational test for nouns (and vice versa). If a personal pronoun can appropriately substitute for a word or group of words, then the word or group of words is functioning as a noun, regardless of its form. This, in turn, obviates the need to teach formally the definitions of noun, noun phrase, and the other constructions which substitute for nouns. If such constructions allow personal pronouns as substitutions in a sentence, then, operationally, they are nouns.

Reliance on this kind of unconscious underlying knowledge of the language, of course, has always been implicit—and crucial—in the development of transformational/generative grammar and its derivative applications for the classroom. It should come as no surprise that the basic design and the general success of sentence-combining exercises rest greatly on this kind of intuitive knowledge. Indeed, without such knowledge, students would be unable to carry out the instructions (i.e., perform the operations) required of such exercises. Yet, with the exception of a small number of studies (D'Eloia 1977; DeBeaugrande 1984a; Noguchi 1987), little has been done to exploit this powerful resource to define grammatical categories for writers, even though the very same resource has been used fruitfully by linguists in their syntactic analyses for the past thirty or so years.

The Underlying Knowledge of "Subject"

An approach capitalizing on intuitive linguistic knowledge can be used to define, for example, the notion of "subject of a sentence." For students, being able to locate the subject of a sentence easily is a valuable skill since several kinds of common stylistic problems require the identification of subjects—for example, errors in subject-verb agreement, unnecessary shifts in person, overuse of nonagent subjects. Locating subjects can most easily be handled by exploiting some descriptive rules of grammar which operate on or interact with subjects. Consider the following declarative sentences and their corresponding tag and yes-no questions:

7. a. Jim and Sue can dance the tango.
   b. Jim and Sue can dance the tango, can't they?
   c. Can Jim and Sue dance the tango?
8. a. The company, which employed many workers and made many different kinds of products, went out of business.
   b. The company, which employed many workers and made many different kinds of products, went out of business, didn't it?
   c. Did the company, which employed many workers and made many different kinds of products, go out of business?
9. a. The cost of the three typewriters and the four clocks will be raised.
   b. The cost of the three typewriters and the four clocks will be raised, won't it?
   c. Will the cost of the three typewriters and the four clocks be raised?
10. a. Tom ate some bad spaghetti and had a stomachache all day.
    b. Tom ate some bad spaghetti and had a stomachache all day, didn't he?
    c. Did Tom eat some bad spaghetti and have a stomachache all day?
11. a. Doing math problems isn't one of Billy's favorite activities.
    b. Doing math problems isn't one of Billy's favorite activities, is it?
    c. Isn't doing math problems one of Billy's favorite activities?
12. a. Whether Sam likes it or not, Janet should telephone David again.
    b. Whether Sam likes it or not, Janet should telephone David again, shouldn't she?

c. Whether Sam likes it or not, should Janet telephone David again?

Forming the corresponding tag and yes-no questions from the original declarative sentences offers a way of identifying subjects operationally. With tag questions (all the (b) sentences above), the pronoun copied at the end of the tag question refers to the subject of the sentence. Stated more simply, the last word of the tag question stands for the subject. For example, in (7b), the last word *they* stands for *Jim and Sue*, the subject of the sentence; in (8b), the last word *it* stands for *the company*; in (9b), *it* stands for *the cost*; in (11b), *it* stands for the whole sequence *doing math problems* (not just *math*), and, hence, the whole sequence is the subject of the sentence. With yes-no questions (all the (c) sentences above), an auxiliary, or "helping," verb has been moved leftward to occupy a new position. If no auxiliary verb occurs in the original declarative sentence, as in (8a) and (10a), an appropriate form of the *do* auxiliary verb (*do, does,* or *did*) is added instead. The subject of the sentence can be identified relative to the new position of the moved or added auxiliary. More specifically, the (simple) subject is the first noun or noun substitute that stands to the immediate right of the moved or added auxiliary verb. Stated more in everyday English, the subject is the first noun or noun substitute that stands to the nearest right of the moved (or added *do*) word. Thus, in (7c), the noun phrase *Jim and Sue* stands to the nearest right of the moved word *can* and, hence, is the subject of the sentence; in (8c), the noun or noun substitute standing to the nearest right of the moved word *did* is *company*; in (9c), the noun or noun substitute standing to the nearest right of the moved word *will* is *cost*.

Handling Some Exceptions

As with any method dealing with the complexities of English grammar, real or apparent exceptions may occur. The key is to explain them as clearly as possible. For example, sentences like (13a) and (14a) will yield a proper corresponding tag question but not a proper corresponding yes-no question:

13. a. For Tommy to pass now isn't going to be easy.
    b. For Tommy to pass now isn't going to be easy, is it?
    c. *Isn't for Tommy to pass now going to be easy?

14. a. That Jane is a genius is obvious to everyone.
    b. That Jane is a genius is obvious to everyone, isn't it?

    c. *Is that Jane is a genius obvious to everyone?

Conversely, a sentence like (15a) will yield a proper corresponding yes-no question but sometimes a noncorresponding (yet proper) tag question:

15. a. I believe that a good education makes a big difference in life.
    b. *I believe that a good education makes a big difference in life, doesn't it? (instead of the syntactically corresponding "I believe that a good education makes a big difference in life, don't I?")
    c. Don't I believe that a good education makes a big difference in life?

The general problem in (13–15) is that the tag question and the yes-no question give conflicting indications of what is the subject of the original sentence. For example, in (13b), the *it* in the tag question refers to or stands for the infinitive phrase *for Tommy to pass now*, and, hence, the whole infinitive phrase is the subject of the sentence. In (13c), however, the yes-no question is corresponding but ungrammatical. To make matters worse, the first noun or noun substitute occurring to the nearest right of the moved word is *Tommy* and, thus, students may incorrectly identify *Tommy*, rather than the whole infinitive phrase *for Tommy to pass now*, as the subject of the sentence.

    Rather than merely viewing the results in (13–15) as contradictory or unrevealing, teachers can exploit such situations not only to sharpen but also to expand their students' skills in employing operational definitions. For example, if in (13b) the last word *it* truly represents a pronominal copy of the subject (i.e., *for Tommy to pass now*), then we ought to be able to substitute *it* for the subject without changing the essential meaning of the sentence. This we can do in both (13a) and (13b) to get *It's not going to be easy* and *It's not going to be easy, is it?*, respectively, thus providing strong evidence that *for Tommy to pass now* is, indeed, the actual subject. Significantly, we can also substitute *it* for the same group of words in the problematic (13c) to get *Isn't it going to be easy?*, again giving strong evidence that *for Tommy to pass now* is the subject of the sentence. (Note that if *Tommy* alone were the subject of the sentence, the corresponding tag question would be the ungrammatical *For Tommy to pass now isn't going to be easy, is he?*). Further analysis, then, shows that the subject of the sentences in (13) is, indeed, the whole infinitive phrase *For Tommy to pass now* rather than just *Tommy* or any other portion of the infinitive phrase. The same line of argument can also be used to explain the discrepancy in identifying the subject in (14).

The discrepancy in (15) can also be explained in a revealing way for students. In (15c), the moved word in the yes-no question correctly indicates that *I* is the subject of the sentence; in (15b), however, the copied pronoun *it* in the tag question refers to *a good education*, and, thus, erroneously indicates that *a good education* is the subject. The cause of the discrepancy here lies more in the *use* of tag questions than in their formation. For example, the tag question that syntactically corresponds to *I believe that a good education makes a big difference in life* is *I believe that a good education makes a big difference in life, don't I?* (If this is offered as a possible tag question to (15a), most, if not all, students will agree.) However, though this is a syntactically correct tag question, we normally do not utter it for reasons having to do with the semantics (i.e., meaning) and pragmatics (i.e., use) of such questions. In contrast to yes-no questions, which seek from the addressee a neutral *yes* or *no* response, tag questions seek a confirmation of whatever the addresser asserts. Put in another way, yes-no questions roughly mean something like, 'My utterance here offers you a free choice. I ask you to indicate the choice with a *yes* or *no*.' Tag questions roughly mean something like, 'My utterance here asserts something. I ask you to confirm or deny the assertion.' In the tag question *I believe that a good education makes a big difference in life, don't I?*, the addresser asserts his or her belief about the importance of a good education in life. However, the meaning of the sentence is strange in that the addresser explicitly affirms his or her own belief (with *I believe*) and then denies or casts doubt on it (with *don't I?*). Because of this conflict between self-affirmation and self-doubt, students often prefer the syntactically noncorresponding tag question *I believe that a good education makes a big difference in life, doesn't it?* We can check this explanation against a comparable tag question, such as *Maria believes that a good education makes a big difference in life, doesn't she?*, which lacks the conflicting beliefs of the addresser and, hence, is more acceptable than **Maria believes that a good education makes a big difference in life, doesn't it?* (Teachers can encourage further exploration of this phenomenon by asking students to substitute other nouns and personal pronouns for the pronoun *I*.) The reason that sentences like (15b) sometimes occur as the tag-question counterparts for sentences like (15a) then is not that students do not know the syntax of tag questions (they do) but rather that they also know something about the semantics and pragmatics (or the meaning and use) of tag questions.

The Importance of Tag-Question and Yes-No Question Formation

What the preceding examples with tag questions and yes-no questions indicate is that students also unconsciously know a great deal more about the categories of English grammar than teachers realize. The very ability to perform the operations of tag-question formation and yes-no question formation presupposes that students already have an underlying knowledge of not only the concept of "subject" but also those of "auxiliary verb," "negative," and "personal pronoun" (and, as we shall see later, also "sentence" and "presentence modifier"). That students have already acquired the concept of personal pronoun (along with the associated concepts of case, number, and gender) is evident in their ability to add the correct noun-equivalent pronoun (with matching case, number, and gender) at the end of the tag question. That students have already acquired the concept of auxiliary verb is evident in their uncanny ability to select, among numerous possibilities within a sentence, the correct word to copy in the tag part of the tag question or the correct word to move leftward in the yes-no question. (The ability to identify auxiliary verbs is further verified when students insert a form of *do* in sentences containing no auxiliary verb. How can they tell that a sentence lacks a movable or copiable auxiliary verb unless they know first what constitutes an auxiliary verb?) That students have already acquired the concept of negative is evident in their ability to add and contract *not* in the tag (or in their ability to negate any positive sentence of English). If students did not possess an underlying knowledge of such categories, they would be unable to produce grammatical tag questions and yes-no questions in everyday conversation.

The Underlying Knowledge of "Main Verb"

The underlying knowledge of native speakers also includes knowledge of the category "main verb." The ability to locate main verbs is important because some highly frequent stylistic errors concern main verbs. These errors involve not only the choice of main verbs (as suggested by the oft-quoted advice, "Write with action verbs") but also their form (incorrect tense, lack of subject-verb agreement, improper tense shifting, nonstandard dialectal forms). Locating the main verb of a sentence, however, is not always easy for students, even when they know the subject of the sentence. Simply asking students, "What is the subject doing?" will not work when, for example, the sentence is passive or the main verb is some form of *be*. Students do, nonetheless, have an underlying knowledge of main verbs. After students have learned how to identify both the subject of a declarative sentence and the correct pronominal form of the subject operationally, teachers can tap their underlying knowledge of main verbs by having students work with sentence frames like A and B below. Frame A isolates the predicate of a sentence in the second slot. If that predicate contains the verb *be*, frame B is then used to separate the linking verb *be* from the passive *be*. In fact, frame B works only with passive sentences and serves to isolate the "real" main verb.

A. They somehow got ＿＿＿＿＿ to ＿＿＿＿＿＿＿＿.

B. But it wasn't me who did the ＿＿＿＿＿-ing.

To locate main verbs with sentence frames A and B, students start with any (declarative) sentence and then use that sentence to fill in the blanks of A and B. The operational test here requires two basic steps:

(1) Insert in the first slot of A the subject of the (declarative) sentence in appropriate pronoun form and insert in the second slot whatever remains of the sentence.

(2) If (and only if) the second slot in A has *be* as the first word, try to fill the slot in B with the appropriate word from the original sentence (this word also has to appear in the second slot in A). If this can't be done, don't worry.

To simplify matters here, sentence negatives may be ignored. Although the sentences produced from following the steps above may sometimes be strange, they will, nonetheless, be sentences (keep in mind that, even in real life, people sometimes utter strange but syntactically correct sentences). More important, the resulting sentences will isolate the main verb in the second slot in A or, if the original sentence is passive, the main verb will appear in the slot in B. The previous declarative sentences in (7–12), repeated for convenience below as (16–21) illustrate the isolation of the main verb. The (a) versions are the original sentences, the (b) versions are the results of using frame A, and the (c) versions show the results of using frame B.

16. a. Jim and Sue can dance the tango.
    b. They somehow got *them* to *dance the tango*. (Hence, *dance* is the main verb.)

17. a. The company, which employed many workers and made many different kinds of products, went out of business.
    b. They somehow got *it* to *go out of business*. (*Go* is the main verb.)

18. a. The cost of the three typewriters and the four clocks will be raised.
    b. They somehow got *it* to *be raised.*
    c. But it wasn't me who did the *raise*-ing. (*Raise* is the main verb.)

19. a. Tom ate some bad spaghetti and had a stomachache all day.
    b. They somehow got *him* to *eat some bad spaghetti and (to) have a stomachache all day.* (Two main verbs here: *eat* and *have.*)

20. a. Doing math problems isn't one of Billy's favorite activities.
    b. They somehow got *it* to *be one of Billy's favorite activities.*
    c. But it wasn't me who did the _____?_____-ing. (Since frame B does not work here, *be* is the main verb.)

21. a. Whether Sam likes it or not, Janet should telephone David again.
    b. They somehow got *her* to *telephone David again, whether Sam likes it or not.* (*Telephone* is the main verb.)

Even the troublesome declarative sentences in (13–15), repeated here as (22–24), yield their main verbs, as indicated below:

22. a. For Tommy to pass now isn't going to be easy.
    b. They somehow got *it* to *be easy.*
    c. But it wasn't me who did the _____?_____-ing. (Hence, *be* is the main verb.)

23. a. That Jane is a genius is obvious to everyone.
    b. They somehow got *it* to *be obvious to everyone.*
    c. But it wasn't me who did the _____?_____-ing. (Hence, *be* is the main verb.)

24. a. I believe that a good education makes a big difference in life.
    b. They somehow got *me* to *believe that a good education makes a big difference in life.* (*Believe* is the main verb.)

As shown by the examples above, sentence frames A and B work together to isolate main verbs from declarative sentences. Sentence frame A isolates transitive and intransitive main verbs from the sentence, while sentence frame B separates the main verb *be* from a passivized main verb (i.e., a main verb which occurs in passive form and which occurs after the auxiliary verb *be*). Working in tandem, sentence frames A and B make the isolation of main verbs considerably easier because they operationally remove distracting auxiliary verbs from consideration as main verbs. For example, the active sentence *Bill could have been taking care of his tired feet* becomes in sentence frame A, *They somehow got him to take care of his tired feet*, while the passive sentence

Mary might have been chosen becomes in sentence frames A and B, *They somehow got her to be chosen* and *But it wasn't me who did the choosing.*

The Underlying Knowledge of "Sentence"

Being able to identify main verbs, main subjects, and auxiliary verbs can, of course, aid students in identifying sentences and defining the all-important notion of "sentence." However, to piece together these elements with others to define a sentence is wasteful of time and effort because native speakers of English already know what a sentence is. That this knowledge already exists, tacit though it may be, is evidenced in the very ability to form grammatical tag questions and yes-no questions. Regardless of the vast numbers of sentences that can be transformed into tag questions or yes-no questions, the key point to keep in mind here is that the operations that form tag questions and yes-no questions work properly only on genuine sentences. While students will have no difficulty in transforming the (a) sentences in (7–12) into tag questions and yes-no questions, they will find the task impossible with such nonsentences as the following:

25. Enjoyed the baseball game on Saturday.
26. Whatever you could do to help my sister.
27. The wind howling through the trees last night.
28. If you came tomorrow afternoon at one o'clock.
29. In order to find a job he liked.

Try as they may, students will find it impossible to form either the corresponding tag question or the corresponding yes-no question for the sequences in (25–29). If forced to write or utter a "corresponding" tag or yes-no question for the sequence in, say, (25), students might come up with one of these constructions:

30. Didn't he enjoy the baseball game on Saturday?
31. Enjoyed the baseball game on Saturday, didn't you?
32. You enjoyed the baseball game on Saturday, didn't you?

Yet even these forced and noncorresponding questions are highly instructive, for they reveal some of the elements which might be added to (25) to make it into a complete sentence. The yes-no question in (30) reveals that (25) lacks a possible *he* subject; the tag questions in (31) and (32) implicitly and explicitly reveal that (25) lacks a possible *you* subject. That is, the very attempt to force a tag question or a yes-no question from a nonsentence offers evidence not only of the existence of a student's underlying knowledge of a (complete) sentence but also the strength of this knowledge.

What ultimately makes tag questions and yes-no questions so useful in differentiating sentences from nonsentences is their ability to mark sentence boundaries. Every sentence, no matter how complex, has two boundaries, one that marks the beginning of the sentence and one that marks its end. (In writing, we can call these two boundaries the left and right boundary, respectively.) Differentiating a sentence from a nonsentence—or, in our terms, defining a sentence operationally—crucially depends upon identifying the two boundaries, since what lies in between them is the sentence. Indeed, one major advantage of using tag-question formation and yes-no question formation as a test for "sentencehood" is that the operations involved visually mark the boundaries of a sentence. Tag-question formation visually marks the right boundary by placing the appropriate tag there (e.g., *isn't he, aren't they*); the yes-no question formation visually marks the left boundary by moving the auxiliary (or adding a *do* form) there. If both boundaries cannot be so marked, then the original sequence falls short of being a sentence.

The following sequences help illustrate the marking of boundaries ("//" indicates a sentence or independent clause boundary):

33. a. // It's a great party //
    b. It's a great party // isn't it?
    c. Is // it _____ a great party?

34. a. // Whatever you say will be okay with Mary //
    b. Whatever you say will be okay with Mary // won't it?
    c. Will // whatever you say _____ be okay with Mary?

35. a. // The man and the woman, neither of whom Ted knows, came from a place called Hamburg //
    b. The man and the woman, neither of whom Ted knows, came from a place called Hamburg // didn't they?
    c. Did // the man and the woman, neither of whom Ted knows, come from a place called Hamburg?

With tag questions, the right sentence boundary is marked even if, for semantic and pragmatic reasons, the wrong subject is copied as the pronoun in the tag, as in (36b) and (37b), or even if the auxiliary verb lacks an accepted negative contracted form, as in (38b) and (39b)[2]:

36. a. // I think Bob is going to Sally's Halloween party in a Dracula costume //

    b. *I think Bob is going to Sally's Halloween party in a Dracula costume // isn't he?

    c. Do // I think Bob is going to Sally's Halloween party in a Dracula costume?

37. a. // We are certain that Janice and her two friends will not get an A in history //

    b. *We are certain that Janice and her two friends will not get an A in history // will they?

    c. Are // we _____ certain that Janice and her two friends will not get an A in history?

38. a. // Dave might finish the assignment over the weekend //

    b. *Dave might finish the assignment over the weekend // mightn't he? (This one is acceptable in certain dialects.)

    c. Might // Dave _____ finish the assignment over the weekend?

39. a. // I'm just being stubborn //

    b. *I'm just being stubborn // am't/ain't I?

    c. Am // I _____ just being stubborn?

With yes-no questions, the left boundary is marked even if the moved element creates an awkward or, to some, an ungrammatical sentence, as in (40c) or (41c):

40. a. // That the rock singer may cut his hair could be a problem //

    b. That the rock singer may cut his hair could be a problem // couldn't it?

    c. Could // that the rock singer may cut his hair _____ be a problem?

41. a. // To be a famous movie star can mean a life without privacy //

    b. To be a famous movie star can mean a life without privacy // can't it?

    c. Can // to be a famous movie star _____ mean a life without privacy?

As one final verification of sentencehood, teachers might enlist students to try a simple operation that is independent of both tag- and yes-no question formation. As all native speakers of English implicitly know (just as all teachers who have used sentence combining as a teaching device explicitly know), sentences can be embedded, or nested, within another. One such embedding environment, or slot, for declarative sentences occurs in (42):

42. They refused to believe the idea that _____.

Although many word sequences will properly fit in the above slot, whatever these sequences are, most of them take the form of a (declarative) sentence. Thus, the (a) sentences in (7–12) can be embedded in (42), as the complex sentences in (43–48) below show:

43. They refused to believe the idea that Jim and Sue can dance the tango.

44. They refused to believe the idea that the company, which employed many workers and made many different kinds of products, went out of business.

45. They refused to believe the idea that the cost of the three typewriters and the four clocks will be raised.

46. They refused to believe the idea that Tom ate some bad spaghetti and had a stomachache all day.

47. They refused to believe the idea that doing math problems isn't one of Billy's favorite activities.

48. They refused to believe the idea that, whether Sam likes it or not, Janet should telephone David again.

In contrast, nonsentence sequences, such as those in (25–29), cannot be embedded in the same environment:

49. *They refused to believe the idea that enjoyed the baseball game on Saturday.

50. *They refused to believe the idea that whatever you could do to help my sister.

51. *They refused to believe the idea that the wind howling through the trees last night.

52. *They refused to believe the idea that if you came tomorrow afternoon at one o'clock.

53. *They refused to believe the idea that in order to find a job he liked.

In most cases, the above method proves easy to use because it provides a controlled syntactic context in which to judge sentence completeness.

The Underlying Knowledge of "Presentence Modifier"

In addition to marking the left boundary of a sentence, yes-no question formation is helpful in identifying presentence modifiers.

Being able to identify these modifiers proves useful in writing since a comma is sometimes required to set off the presentence modifier from the rest of the sentence.[3] Although appearing in various forms and lengths, all presentence modifiers share two syntactic characteristics: they occur, as the grammatical terminology suggests, at the beginning of the sentence, and they are movable to some other location in the sentence, whether it be the end or somewhere in the middle (the exact position is unimportant here). The basic problem of identifying presentence modifiers, or really separating them from the rest of the sentence, lies in the variety of forms they take. They can be a word, a phrase, or a clause. The value of yes-no question formation lies in its ability to treat them all alike syntactically. If a presentence modifier occurs in a declarative sentence, yes-no question formation will either place the moved auxiliary to its right or displace the modifier to some other location in the sentence. (The displacement of the modifier occurs because of stylistic reasons and is not a part of the yes-no question rule itself.) In either case, the presentence modifier becomes easily identifiable. The presentence modifier is either everything in the sentence that stands to the left of the moved auxiliary verb (or added *do* form) or everything that moves rightward to some other position in the sentence. The following sentences, containing a variety of presentence modifiers, illustrate the point (the modifiers under consideration are in italics for easy reference):

54. a. *Frankly,* everyone says that my fifth-grade teacher is mean.
    b. *Frankly,* does everyone say that my fifth-grade teacher is mean?
    c. Does everyone say, *frankly,* that my fifth-grade teacher is mean?

55. a. *Consequently,* the whole street was destroyed by the tornado.
    b. *Consequently,* was the whole street destroyed by the tornado?
    c. Was the whole street, *consequently,* destroyed by the tornado?

56. a. *In Los Angeles about this time,* Janine claimed that she saw a flying saucer zoom over her house.
    b. *In Los Angeles about this time,* did Janine claim that she saw a flying saucer zoom over her house?
    c. Did Janine claim that *in Los Angeles about this time* she saw a flying saucer zoom over her house?

57. a. *Things being what they are,* Jerry's mother is very angry at him.
    b. *Things being what they are,* is Jerry's mother very angry at him?
    c. Is Jerry's mother very angry at him, *things being what they are?*

58. a. *Although he has never hit a home run in his life,* Jeremy still loves
        to play baseball.
    b. *Although he has never hit a home run in his life,* does Jeremy still
       love to play baseball?
    c. Does Jeremy still love to play baseball, *although he has never hit
       a home run in his life?*
59. a. *When the food arrives,* we'll start with the pepperoni pizza first.
    b. *When the food arrives,* will we start with the pepperoni pizza
       first?
    c. Will we start with the pepperoni pizza first *when the food arrives?*

Pedagogically, the main benefit of using the yes-no question to
identify presentence modifiers lies in avoiding the laborious and time-
consuming chore of presenting all the various types of presentence
modifiers. Teachers need not introduce individually such modifiers as
adverbial disjuncts, conjunctive adverbs, prepositional phrases, nominative absolutes, and adverbial clauses; nor need teachers differentiate between one-word, phrasal, or clausal modifiers. Syntactically
blind to such distinctions, yes-no question formation operationally
defines presentence modifiers in one general and easily perceptible
way: they either occur to the left of the moved auxiliary or added *do*
form or else they get moved from the presentence position.

The Applicability of the Basic Categories

We have now operationally defined a set of basic categories—subject,
verb (both main and auxiliary), (presentence) modifier, and sentence
(or independent clause). If we take into account other categories that
become transparent in tag-question formation, we may supplement
the basic set with (personal) pronoun, noun, noun phrase and noun
substitute, and negative. While the foregoing categories are by no
means all the categories that we might define operationally, they
comprise a fundamental set for identifying and correcting many
highly frequent and sometimes highly stigmatized kinds of errors. In
reducing these errors, some of these categories constitute a starting
point; for others, they constitute the crucial category (or categories).
The importance and potential utility of these categories become
clearer if we distribute them in relation to Connors and Lunsford's
(1988) list of the twenty most frequent formal errors:

1. No comma after introductory element (presentence modifier,
   sentence)

2. Vague pronoun reference (pronoun, noun, noun phrase, noun substitute)
3. No comma in compound sentence (independent clause)
4. Wrong word
5. No comma in nonrestrictive element
6. Wrong/missing inflected endings (verb, noun)
7. Wrong or missing preposition
8. Comma splice (sentence or independent clause)
9. Possessive apostrophe error
10. Tense shift (main verb, auxiliary verb)
11. Unnecessary shift in person (possibly subject or pronoun)
12. Sentence fragment (sentence or independent clause)
13. Wrong tense or verb form (main verb, auxiliary verb)
14. Subject-verb agreement (subject, auxiliary verb, main verb)
15. Lack of comma in series
16. Pronoun agreement error (pronoun, subject, main verb, auxiliary verb)
17. Unnecessary comma with restrictive element
18. Run-on or fused sentence (sentence or independent clause)
19. Dangling or misplaced modifier (presentence modifier, sentence)
20. Its/it's error

The importance and potential utility of these categories also become more apparent when they are placed in relation to Hairston's (1981) "status marking" and "very serious" errors, the two most stigmatized kinds of stylistic errors:

Status Marking

nonstandard verb forms in past or past participle (verb)

lack of subject-verb agreement: *We was* instead of *We were; Jones don't think it's acceptable* instead of *Jones doesn't think it's acceptable* (subject, main verb, auxiliary verb)

double negatives (negative)

objective pronoun as subject (pronoun, subject)

Very Serious

sentence fragments (sentence or independent clause)

run-on sentences (sentence or independent clause)

noncapitalization of proper nouns (noun)

would of instead of *would have* (possibly auxiliary verb)

lack of subject-verb agreement, non–status marking (subject, auxiliary verb, main verb)

insertion of comma between the verb and its complement (main verb)

nonparallelism

faulty adverb forms

use of transitive verb *set* for intransitive *sit* (verb)

The Practical Benefits

Isolating basic categories of grammar in the manner demonstrated here, then, produces practical benefits. Aside from its relevance to correcting some highly frequent and stigmatized errors, the method reduces significantly the time expended on grammar instruction.[4] Teachers need not present to students all the customary grammatical categories, only a small set of them. Second, and as a direct result of the first benefit, it creates more time to devote to other matters of writing. While unconventional features of style need attention at some point in writing instruction, they should not be the sole nor the primary area of attention. Third, because the method demonstrated here relies on a body of already acquired knowledge, it requires less effort to present the basic categories. Teachers present—and students apply—what they already unconsciously know. Fourth, the method ties in nicely with a process approach to writing. Just as students can improve paragraphs and whole essays by learning about and partaking more consciously in the process of writing, so too can they improve their sentence mechanics by learning about and partaking more consciously in the process (i.e., the operations) of sentence formation.

Notes

1. The asterisk here denotes an ungrammatical sentence, that is, one which violates the descriptive rules of English grammar.

2. When working with tag-question formation, instructors will sooner or later encounter word sequences which are genuine sentences but which, on first try, cannot be transformed into grammatical tag questions (at least not in

all regional or social varieties of English). These cases involve sentences containing modal verbs (a subclass of auxiliary verbs) like *may, might, ought,* and *shall,* which, if contracted with *not,* produce in some dialects or styles the unacceptable **mayn't, *mightn't, *oughtn't,* and **shalln't (shalln't* [or *shan't*], for example, being unacceptable in many non-British dialects), or the main or auxiliary verb form *am* (which, if contracted with *not,* results in the unacceptable *amn't*). Although such verbs may not contract with *not* to form grammatical tag questions, in some varieties of English they do appear in *uncontracted* form in tag questions. Thus, for example, *He might come tomorrow* can be transformed into *He might come tomorrow, might he not?* (or, possibly, *He might come tomorrow, might not he?*). Although the resulting tag question is formal in style, it is, nonetheless, in some varieties of English, a grammatical—and corresponding—tag question. To keep matters simple, instructors should, whenever appropriate, inform students that, if the inability to contract the verb is the *only* problem in forming the proper tag question, then the proper tag question is a formal one (i.e., one with an uncontracted verb in the tag part of the question). One other point needs mentioning. Even though verb forms like *may, might, ought, shall,* and *am* may not be contracted with the negative in some varieties of English, so strong is the pattern to have a contracted verb in tag questions (assuming, of course, the original sentence is positive) that native speakers of English will often substitute for an uncontractable verb a contractable one and usually one that's similar in meaning or time reference. Thus, in informal styles, the following changes will occur: *may, might* → *won't; ought* → *shouldn't; shall* → *won't; am* → *aren't, ain't.* Teachers and students should view such changes solely as efforts of English speakers to get around the uncontractability problem mentioned above.

3. Some handbooks state that the comma should be inserted only if the introductory phrase or clause is a "long" one, usually set arbitrarily at five or more words; however, students who add a comma even for "short" introductory phrases and clauses can hardly go wrong, given the arbitrariness of what constitutes "long." If students realize that all presentence modifiers are also fragments, then a more general and more acceptable rule is possible: "When a fragment immediately precedes a (genuine) sentence and both are intended to be read as one unit, the fragment is set off from the sentence by a comma." The greatest advantage of this rule is that instructors do not need to define the various kinds of phrases (e.g., prepositional, participial, infinitive) or the various kinds of dependent clauses (e.g., adverbial). When a fragment immediately *follows* a (genuine) sentence and both are intended to be read as one unit, the fragment is often (not always) set off by a comma.

4. Using the same underlying principles but slightly different operational syntactic tests than the ones outlined in this study, DeBeaugrande (1984a) reports impressive results in getting college students to identify subjects, number-carrying verbs, verb tenses, and fragments. For example, he states that, with respect to identifying subjects and predicates, posttest scores showed an improvement of approximately 500 percent over pretest scores (363); the same study found that forty-five students who had been taught an operational test for identifying number-carrying verbs and verb tenses made less than half as many errors in recognition than before treatment (365).

My own work with the approach based on underlying syntactic knowledge shows less spectacular gains but highly favorable responses from teachers who use the approach. In the fall of 1988, I conducted a study which differed significantly from DeBeaugrande's insofar as it contrasted two approaches (i.e., a traditional or conventional approach versus the approach based on underlying syntactic knowledge) and covered a wider range of students with greater variability in writing skills, specifically, one sixth-grade elementary school class, three ninth-grade junior high classes, and two freshman-level and two developmental-writing college classes. As a means of identifying fragments, run-ons, and comma splices, the participating teachers (all of whom taught multiple classes or sections) taught a traditional (usually a traditional grammar) approach to one set of students and the approach based on underlying syntactic knowledge to another set of students. On the basis of pretests and posttests, the experimental groups (i.e., students taught the approach based on underlying syntactic knowledge) showed about the same positive gains in identifying fragments, run-ons, and comma splices as the control groups (i.e., students taught a traditional approach). At the least, the results indicated that students generally do benefit from exposure to some grammar instruction, whether formal or informal, in identifying the three kinds of sentencing errors. In all likelihood, the lack of differentiation in the results of the two approaches lay in two substantial factors: (1) because the experimental and control groups in the study generally could not be equalized with respect to academic ability without severely disrupting the teachers' normal conduct of classes, the higher-achieving class was always assigned as the control group and the lower-achieving class (or classes) as the experimental group, and (2) because most students in the study reported that they had studied traditional grammar for many years, the control groups (both students and teachers) generally had much more exposure and practice with the traditional method than the experimental groups had with the new approach. Yet, despite the probable influence of these two factors, many students in the experimental groups made significant gains, some comparable to those reported by DeBeaugrande. The most impressive findings, however, lay in teachers' responses to the approach based on underlying syntactic knowledge. An attitudinal questionnaire completed by the five teachers who participated in the study and by three other teachers who had also used the approach during the same period generally showed favorable or highly favorable responses with respect to ease of presentation, economy of time, and overall impression. Further, all believed strongly or very strongly that they could get better results with more practice, and all strongly or very strongly indicated that they planned to use the approach in future writing classes (the latter item on the questionnaire, in fact, received the highest positive score of all, with seven out of eight teachers indicating "very strongly"). Lastly and somewhat strangely, a majority of instructors (five out of seven) perceived the experimental method as bringing better results than traditional methods, even though their students, on the average, made about the same gains with the experimental method as with the conventional method. In light of the other responses to the questionnaire, a likely explanation here is that these instructors interpreted "better results" in the questionnaire item "Did the USK [i.e., the Underlying Syntactic Knowledge] method bring better results than the method(s) you normally use?" to mean better results with respect to time and effort spent. (I wish to thank Jeffrie Ahmad, Linda Beauregard-Vasquez, Pamela Grove, Lynn McDonie, John Peters, Mary Riggs, Ilene

Rubenstein, and Anne Lise Schofield for their aid in completing this study.)

Positive responses to the underlying-syntactic-knowledge method also come from students themselves. In a study of developmental writers conducted at Antelope Valley College, Beauregard-Vasquez (1989) found that students who were taught the underlying-syntactic-knowledge method not only made 40.5 percent fewer errors in identifying fragments and 37.9 percent fewer errors in identifying run-ons and comma splices but also, with much less classroom instruction, made greater average gains than a control group taught only traditional grammar. Just as important, students greatly preferred the underlying-syntactic-knowledge method over traditional grammar instruction. On the basis of narrative student evaluations of the method, Beauregard-Vasquez states that students found the underlying-syntactic-knowledge method to be a "fun" and "easy" way to "fix" their papers and that students wished that they had learned the method earlier, or in the words of one student:

> I have gone to many English classes all through my years of school, and I have been taught the same type of skills. . . . But the tag and yes-no question method is by far the most unique and simplified method I have ever been taught. . . . I like the method because it is something new and exciting. It is far better than anything else they tried to teach me. (16)

Beauregard-Vasquez notes that the method seems to give students a greater sense of confidence and helps reduce the "excessive blame they tend to place on themselves for not already knowing grammar," or as stated by another student:

> I'm very excited about this new way of learning grammar. I've always felt that I was the problem when it came to learning; however, I thought that it was a lack of attention or just being unable to soak up the material. But now I know it's not; in fact, it was never me. It was the way the material was presented. (15)

4 Run-ons, Comma Splices, and Native-Speaker Abilities

For teachers of writing, probably no stylistic error creates as much frustration as run-ons and comma splices. By a "run-on" or a "run-on sentence" (or alternatively, a "fused sentence"), I mean a sequence of two or more sentences written as one, with no punctuation between the independent clauses (e.g., *Jack and his relatives plan to visit Disneyland they leave next Wednesday*). By a "comma splice," I mean two or more sentences written as one, with a comma joining the independent clauses (e.g., *Jack and his relatives plan to visit Disneyland, they leave next Wednesday*). Run-ons and comma splices occur at all grade levels, from elementary school to college and even beyond. Parris (n.d., 1), in "Sisyphus and the Comma Splice," states, "The comma splice, for years, was the most frequent violation of traditional punctuation rules I encountered, a violation committed by my students at all levels, whether in freshman composition, advanced expository, or upper-level business and technical writing classes." Connors and Lunsford (1988), in their study of the twenty most frequently occurring formal errors in college writing, place comma splices eighth and run-ons eighteenth. At the elementary and secondary school level, run-ons and comma splices, in all likelihood, occur with even greater frequency. If for no other reason than their relatively high degree of occurrence and their problematic character, run-ons and comma splices deserve scrutiny, particularly with respect to their status as errors, their causes and, most important, their remedies.

The Problems in Treating Run-ons and Comma Splices

Finding a way to eliminate run-ons and comma splices presents a formidable challenge, not just for the operational approach presented in this study, but for any approach designed to improve sentence mechanics. The pedagogical problems are both obvious and daunting. If run-ons and comma splices, by definition, consist of two or more independent clauses misjoined by incorrect or no punctuation, the problem is made at least doubly difficult by the fact that treatment requires the isolation of not just one independent clause but two or more of them in sequence—and without the help of punctuation and capitalization (since they are incorrect to begin with). To make matters worse, an effective remedy must not only provide a means of identifying independent clauses but also an easy way of locating the point of illicit merger so that the appropriate punctuation can be added. Finally and worst of all, run-ons and comma splices require recognition of the grammatical category "sentence" or "independent clause," by far the most complex of all syntactic categories. As many teachers can attest, a sentence or an independent clause is not a structure which can be easily and transparently defined for students.

Traditional definitions of a clause or a sentence prove opaque or, at best, unwieldy because of their vagueness or their interlinkage with definitions of other grammatical categories. For example, defining a sentence as a sequence of words having "a complete thought" only shifts the problem to the equally perplexing task of defining "a complete thought." Defining a sentence as a unit with a complete subject and complete predicate (or, alternatively, with a noun-phrase subject and a verb phrase), necessitates defining "subject" and "predicate" (not to mention the notion of "complete") and eventually "noun," "verb," and probably "verb complement" (e.g., direct object, indirect object). What starts off as a seemingly simple task of defining a sentence results in rapidly proliferating definitions of the parts of the sentence, with the misunderstanding of any one of the parts likely to lead to the misunderstanding of the whole.

Five Kinds of Native-Speaker Abilities

If the pedagogical task of defining a sentence were not vexing enough, the problem of run-ons and comma splices becomes all the more frustrating if we consider that run-ons and comma splices seem to be errors that ought not to occur in the first place, at least not among native speakers of English. Native speakers of English, by virtue of being native speakers, have the following linguistic abilities:

1. The ability to distinguish a grammatical sentence from an ungrammatical one: e.g., *The cook put the soup on the stove* versus **The cook put the soup* or **Cook the put soup the on stove the*

2. The ability to produce and understand an infinite number of new sentences of potentially infinite length: e.g., *Jack went home, and he fixed himself a sandwich, and he cleaned his room, and he turned on his stereo, and. . . .*

3. The ability to recognize ambiguous sentences: e.g., *My mother hates boring guests* (i.e., 'My mother hates to bore guests' or 'My mother hates guests who are boring').

4. The ability to recognize synonymous sentences: e.g., *Alice and Tom washed the car* versus *The car was washed by Alice and Tom.*

5. The ability to recognize the internal structure of sentences: e.g., *Julia is eager to help* versus *Julia is easy to help.* (In the first sentence, Julia does the helping; in the second sentence, someone helps Julia.)

If native (but not non-native) speakers of English already possess the prodigious syntactic and semantic abilities illustrated in (1–5), then what becomes especially puzzling—and frustrating—is that these very abilities all hinge on a knowledge of what constitutes a sentence, precisely the knowledge which seems lacking in students who write with run-ons and comma splices (and fragments). That is, whatever run-ons and comma splices are, they, as written units, constitute nonsentences of the language.

Native-speaker knowledge of what constitutes a sentence is illustrated explicitly in (1) above. Native speakers of English will all agree that the first sequence (*The cook put the soup on the stove*) is a grammatical (i.e., genuine) sentence of English; however, no native speaker will argue the same for the second and third sequences (**The cook put the soup* and **Cook the put soup the on stove the*). Strictly speaking, these two sequences, though they consist of English words, are nonsentences of English. (Following established convention, I will continue to refer to such nonsentence sequences as ungrammatical "sentences.") If a non-native speaker of English were to utter in conversation, "The cook put the soup," a native speaker of English would immediately recognize the utterance not only as a nonsentence sequence but also as a nonsentence sequence lacking something at the end which would turn it into a genuine sentence. More specifically, the native speaker would know that the correct use of the verb *put* requires, among other things, an indication of location or place. Relying on these native-speaker intuitions, the native speaker upon hearing "The cook put the soup," might ask, "Put the soup where?"

While (1) focuses directly on a native speaker's ability to distinguish a sentence of English from a nonsentence of English, (2–5) indirectly assume this ability. Take, for example, the ability to produce and understand an infinite number of new sentences of potentially infinite length. Native speakers could not, in principle, produce an infinite number of new sentences (and only sentences) or sentences of infinite length if they first did not know what entities they were creating (i.e., sentences). To produce any kind of entity (and only that entity) in limitless number or variety, the producers must first have a basic understanding of what that entity is; otherwise, they could not, except by pure accident, produce variations of that entity. Similarly, native speakers cannot recognize an ambiguous sentence until they interpret the meaning of the whole sentence—a task which first requires knowing what a sentence is. If we pursue the same line of argument, native speakers cannot render appropriate judgment on whether a pair of sentences is synonymous or not without first ascertaining that the two sequences are indeed sentences. That is, while *Alice and Tom washed the car* is synonymous to *The car was washed by Alice and Tom*, it is not synonymous to the nonsentence sequences *Car washed the by Alice and Tom was* or *The washing of the car by Alice and Tom*. Finally, the ability to recognize the internal structure of sentences presupposes that native speakers know what entity to look within to find the "inner" structure. That entity is, of course, the sentence.

If native speakers already possess abilities 1–5 and if these abilities require or presuppose a prior knowledge of what constitutes a sentence, then run-ons, comma splices (and fragments) seem to comprise a far different kind of error than prescriptive, or usage, errors like ending a sentence with a preposition, splitting an infinitive, using *hopefully* as a sentence modifier, or using *ain't*. To make this difference clearer, consider the usage errors in the following sequences:

1. The neighbors didn't know what country the family came from.
2. To quickly act during emergencies can save lives.
3. Hopefully, it will not rain during our baseball game.
4. Bert and Henry ain't goin' to church today.
5. *Bert and Henry goin' ain't to church today.

In contrast to run-ons and comma splices, the usage errors contained in the first four sequences do not centrally involve abilities associated with being a native speaker of the language. The first sequence, despite the sentence-ending preposition, is still a possible sentence of English. The same holds for the second and third sequences, despite the split infinitive (*To quickly act*) and the use of *hopefully* as a sentence adverbial. Even the fourth sequence, with socially stigmatized *ain't* and the reduced ending of *going*, still qualifies as a bona fide sentence of the language. Although some fastidious native speakers may protest that the first four sequences contain improprieties, none would claim that they are "non-English" sentences. While (1–4) may contain certain violations, these violations concern linguistic etiquette (i.e., the social use of language), not violations of sentence formation (i.e., infractions of descriptive rules) and, thus, are judged as genuine sentences of the language. Sequence 5, in contrast, does involve a violation of a rule of sentence formation. Although consisting of English words, *Bert and Henry goin' ain't to church today* would be viewed by all native speakers as a nonsentence of English, not because it contains *ain't* or *goin'*, but because it violates the sentence-formation rule (a descriptive rule) that the auxiliary verb and its contracted negative (here *ain't*) always precede the main verb, not follow it.

A Curious Paradox and Its Repercussions

If native writers, by virtue of being native speakers of English, possess the ability to produce and recognize what constitutes a legitimate sentence of their language, then we confront a curious paradox with run-ons and comma splices. The paradox can be stated somewhat expansively as follows: native writers frequently write with run-ons and comma splices, which, by definition, are not genuine sentences; yet, given that these writers already know and can recognize sentences of English by being native speakers of English, such errors should not occur, or, at least, not with the frequency that they do. The source of the errors cannot lie in speakers' not knowing the correct end product. While writers may commit usage errors—such as ending a sentence with a preposition, splitting an infinitive, using *hopefully* as a sentence modifier, or using *ain't*—they usually do so because they do not realize that such features may violate some prescriptive rules of writing. That is, given the choice of writing *Hopefully, it will not rain during our baseball game* or *We hope it will not rain during our baseball game* or *It is hoped that it will not rain during our baseball game*, these students most likely would not know, without formal instruction, which sentence violates the prescriptive rule. These same students, by virtue of being native speakers of English, however, would readily recognize without formal instruction that *The cook put the soup on the stove* is a legitimate sentence of English while *The cook put the soup* is not.

That native-writer run-ons and comma splices seem to run counter to the very notion of native speakerhood helps explain, to some extent, not only the high degree of frustration they create but also their high degree of stigma. Hairston, in her survey of reactions to nonstandard writing features among nonacademic professionals, places comma splices in a group of errors she labels "moderately serious," but run-ons and fragments fall in a group of errors she labels "very serious." That such features in formal written discourse often evoke harsh criticism among professionals, nonacademic and academic, comes as no surprise if we consider the importance and centrality that the educational establishment and most educated readers bestow on the sentence in formal writing. In the eyes of the professional public, sentences constitute the building blocks of formal writing; that is, formal written discourse is composed of or at least constructed from well-formed (i.e., genuine) sentences. Formal writing containing such nonsentence sequences as unintentional run-ons, comma splices, and fragments, however, strikes at the very heart of this strongly held belief. Hence, native writers who write with run-ons, comma splices, and fragments encounter far harsher condemnation than non-native writers. (Indeed, the only native writers exempt from harsh criticism here are very young writers—preschool or elementary school level— who are in the beginning stages of acquiring the conventions of writing.) To recapitulate briefly, because native writers should already possess the ability to produce and recognize genuine sentences of the language, run-ons and comma splices (and fragments) ought not to occur in formal writing; however, because such errors do occur with native writers and because the professional public believes the primary unit of formal writing to be the sentence, sentence-boundary errors, like run-ons and comma splices, often elicit a higher degree of censure than many kinds of usage errors.

So strong is the belief that native speakers ought to know and use sentences in verbal communication that some researchers have strongly (but wrongly) implicated "verbal deprivation" or a "language deficit" for those who don't. For example, on the basis of oral interviews with young African American children, Bereiter et al. (1966) describe the language of African American children as that of gestures and "single words" and "a series of badly connected words or phrases" and baldly state that "these four-year-olds could make no statements of any kind" (114). After presumably training these children to "operate at the statement level," the same researchers claim that what experienced teachers of culturally disadvantaged children find the most impressive achievement of these children is "the fact that they speak in sentences" (121–22). (For convincing rebuttal of this study, see Labov 1969.) Significantly, Basil Bernstein's notion of "public language," an earlier version of his "restricted code" (a socially learned and, according to Bernstein, an educationally disadvantageous style of speaking) is characterized by, among other features, "short, grammatically simple, often unfinished sentences"

(1971, 42). Leaving aside questions of accuracy and validity (and they are considerable), these studies suggest, among other things, that the structural unit "sentence" is considered so basic that frequent use of nonsentence sequences in certain discourse situations may result in unfavorable and sometimes unfounded assessments of native-speaking language abilities, even to the point of positing pathological or cultural deprivation.

Resolving the Paradox

Why is it that native speakers of English, despite their native-language abilities, frequently write with run-ons and comma splices, or, put somewhat cryptically, why is it that native speakers, who ought to know better, don't? Part of the answer probably lies in what causes many other types of writing errors, that is, inattention, carelessness, even laziness. However, I also believe that a large part of the answer, perhaps the largest, lies in some crucial physical differences between speech and writing. While both modes of communication use a system of verbal symbols to convey virtually any kind of message (from philosophical treatises to sweet nothings), writing is distinguished from speech by, among other things, different conventions to mark sentence boundaries. Where speech utilizes phonological signals (intonation and pauses) to mark sentence boundaries, writing usually marks these boundaries graphologically with an initial capital letter and appropriate end punctuation (e.g., a period or a question mark). This has been the prevailing method of marking sentence boundaries in standard written English, including and perhaps particularly, formal expository writing. When writers produce run-ons and comma splices, however, they, knowingly or unknowingly, violate this writing convention, or put in another way, the phonological sentence does not coincide with the graphological sentence. (See Bamberg 1977 for one possible way to increase writer awareness of the phonological sentence.)

While the boundary markings of the phonological sentence have probably remained constant throughout the history of English, the same cannot be said of the graphological sentence. Indeed, from what language historians can gather from the punctuation of early written texts, today's run-ons and comma splices (and fragments) may not have been infelicities at all in centuries past. W. F. Bolton (1982) points out that Old English not only had different writing conventions but that these conventions varied so much among individual writers that extracting a set of commonly shared conventions proves, if not impossible, at least difficult. He writes, "The only mark of punctuation in the *Beowulf* manuscript was the period, and that appeared rarely; when it did, it was almost always at the end of the verse line; the same was true of many early Chaucer manuscripts: they were punctuated only with the period, and it appeared only at the end of the verse lines, whether or not a sentence ended there. . . . The manuscripts of Wyclif [i.e., John Wycliffe, c. 1330–84] were more heavily punctuated, but the system of punctuation was not ours" (177–78). Bolton adds that, in Wycliffe's remarks on the Lord's Prayer (Matthew 6:14–15), he begins the second sentence with a capital letter but not the first (178). Punctuation of formal written discourse two hundred years after Wycliffe still shows significant differences from today's conventions. Walter J. Ong (1944) argues that late sixteenth- and early seventeenth-century punctuation was a mixture of two systems, neither of them identical to the modern system, one being a system based on elocution and the other based on an earlier tradition in which the punctuation indicated "neither the syntax nor the niceties of delivery, but is rather a device serving primarily the exigencies of breathing in discourse, considered basically as oral, with due respect only secondarily for the demands of sense" (354–55). All this is not to claim that students who write without sentence-initial capital letters and sentence-final punctuation write like Chaucer, Wycliffe, or the *Beowulf* poet, but these students do share one fact with writers of earlier periods, namely, that their conventions for marking sentence boundaries differ from today's written standard.

Interestingly, remnants of the earlier traditions of marking sentence boundaries still persist among beginning writers. I do not wish to suggest here that beginning writers have some kind of clairvoyant access to earlier writing conventions; however, since the earlier systems of punctuation have their roots in speech, and given that beginning writers often view writing as just a transcription of speech, it is highly likely, indeed probable, that their unconventional system of punctuation reproduces, to some extent, part of the earlier systems. For instance, today's system of marking sentence boundaries is based essentially on syntactic form (i.e., the presence of independent clauses). Earlier tradition, as suggested by Bolton and Ong, first relied primarily on the necessity of breathing and, later, more on meaning and rhetorical effect ("elocution"). If we look at Irene Brosnahan's (1976) "A Few Good Words for the Comma Splice," particularly her criteria for permissible comma splices—criteria based, she claims, on actual usage of writers—the connection to earlier traditions, particularly to one based on meaning, becomes more apparent:

Rule: The comma alone is used to separate independent clauses, without any accompanying conjunction, under the following conditions:

1. Syntax—the clauses are short and usually parallel in structure though they can be in any combination of affirmative and negative clauses.
2. Semantics—the sentence cannot be potentially ambiguous, and the semantic relationship between the clauses is paraphrase, repetition, amplification, opposition, addition, or summary.
3. Style—the usage level is General English or Informal English.
4. Rhetorical—the effect is rapidity of movement and/or emphasis. (185)

Where Brosnahan's main rule and first condition reflect a syntactic basis for determining acceptable comma splices, the other conditions reflect more a meaning basis (cognitive, social, and rhetorical) and hence connect more closely to an earlier system of punctuation. If students do, in fact, produce and punctuate run-ons and comma splices on the basis of these conditions, as Brosnahan suggests, then it would not seem implausible to claim that some beginning writers reproduce or, perhaps, better, continue a historically earlier tradition that was institutionally supplanted but never completely died. Significantly, the historic development of a semantically based punctuation system into a syntactically based one is found ontologically in the way young children acquire the present system, or, as Patricia Cordeiro states, "Meaning structures are not bounded by orthographic structures or syntactic sentences. Children, in attempting to learn how to punctuate the ongoing stream of writing are in actual fact learning a new form of language organization: the sentence" (1988, 72).

We should not, however, be led to believe that students who have already learned how to read but who write with run-ons and comma splices are completely unaware of the syntactically based system of marking sentence boundaries. To dispel this erroneous view, we need only to cite the greater number of correctly demarcated graphological sentences that usually do appear in their writing. If students possessed no knowledge whatsoever of the syntactically based system, the latter sentences would be unlikely to occur in such high frequency. I suspect, however, that, during the multifaceted task of putting words on paper, students who know the syntactically based system yet write with run-ons and comma errors allow the syntactically based system to recede from immediate consciousness, thus making it easier for the competing, and in many ways more natural and more expressive, semantically based system to exert itself. Note how readily and frequently even skilled writers, during the onrush of ideas, merge into one sentence what should be two separate sentences or how these same writers punctuate what are clearly (i.e., syntactically) questions with periods. Stated in another way, the surge or grip of ideas sometimes proves strong enough to override the constraints of form. If we think along these lines, it is no accident that Brosnahan's first condition, the only syntactically based condition, would lead writers to punctuate two short parallel clauses as one. In fact, we could justifiably reinterpret Brosnahan's one syntactic condition as a semantic one. In her first condition, Brosnahan specifically states that the two merged clauses are "short and usually parallel in structure." However, in accordance with our line of argument, writers of run-ons and comma splices can plausibly view anything parallel in structure as being parallel in meaning. That is, given that writers normally compose with meanings rather than contentless form, writers can just as readily perceive the two clauses semantically (in terms of parallel ideas) rather than syntactically (in terms of parallel structure). When the semantic bond of the parallel ideas becomes stronger than the syntactic bond of the parallel constructions, meaning considerations override syntactic form and thus also override boundaries of the syntactic sentence. That the two merged clauses are "short" also has bearing on the production of run-ons and comma splices. Given that writers are more likely to compose and/or perceive parallel ideas in two short sequences than in two long ones, and that writers are, generally, more likely to merge two short sequences than two long ones, it should come as no great surprise that Brosnahan's first condition also turns out to be the most common condition under which run-ons and comma splices occur.

Obviously, the larger picture that emerges from the preceding discussion concerns a clash of writing criteria, either historically or developmentally, with differing evaluations of sentence boundaries depending on who the writers are, when they wrote, and why. Within this larger picture, it becomes clearer that run-ons and comma splices, far from being mere instances of random error, reveal writers' efforts to organize meaning, albeit in a way which violates present writing conventions for marking sentence boundaries. Moreover, it seems that writers at all levels encounter an institutionally extinct but developmentally latent and powerful semantically based system for punctuating sentences.

A Proper Perspective on Run-ons and Comma Splices

From a strictly practical perspective, how should teachers view run-ons and comma splices in light of the misconceptions that seem to surround them? For one thing, teachers need to keep in mind that good writing can and should accommodate intentional nonsentence sequences. A skilled writer might deliberately (and iconically) use a comma splice to convey a closely connected series of events (e.g., *We came, we saw, we conquered*) or a run-on to create a sense of prolixity and mechanical prattle (as in e.e. cummings's poem "next to of course god america i") or a sentence fragment to create emphasis and a sense of informality (as in many contemporary magazine advertisements). Brosnahan (1976) argues for other writing situations where comma splices might be contextually appropriate, as do Kline and Memering (1977) for the sentence fragment.

Second, teachers need to keep in mind that unintentional run-ons and comma splices, even if they occur in large numbers, are not indicators of a defective concept of the sentence, at least, not among native writers. Writers, particularly developing ones, will write with run-ons and comma splices as they experiment with more complex structures in the written medium, but these errors may indicate a transitional stage of development. Teachers especially will have to guard against the view that run-ons and comma splices signal a defective linguistic competence. While intentional and contextually appropriate run-ons and comma splices usually escape censure and may even evoke praise, unintentional ones are often singled out, at best, as symptoms of careless or sloppy writing and, at worst, as symptoms of a language deficit (i.e., an incomplete or incorrect learning of one's native language). Although the production of a greater number of genuine sentences than run-ons and comma splices should warn against a language-deficit explanation, such evidence often goes unnoticed or ignored. Instead, for a considerable number of teachers, the language-deficit explanation gains all the more credence when run-ons and comma splices continue to appear with high frequency in writing even after formal instruction on how to identify and remove them. The thinking seems to run thus: because these students are native speakers of English, they should know what a sentence is; yet some continually write with run-ons and comma splices, even after grammar lessons; although I'm sure they're native speakers of English, the many run-ons and comma splices show clearly that they don't know where one sentence ends and the next one begins; therefore, they really don't know what a sentence is. The next step, of course, is to brand the students' native knowledge of English as defective. Yet, as Chomsky (1959, 1965), Lenneberg (1967), McNeill (1970), and other linguistic researchers have convincingly argued, all human beings are not only biologically equipped and predisposed to learn a native language, but, more important here, they acquire it completely and perfectly. It is not only unnatural but inconceivable that native speakers would acquire the linguistic ability to produce, for example, commands but not questions—or, along the same lines, noun phrases or verb phrases but not sentences.

As the foregoing suggests, the problem of run-ons and comma splices is exacerbated by native-speaker abilities—what all native speakers already unconsciously know as bona fide speakers of the language—failing to meet the demands of the written medium. If they're native speakers, writers ought to know already what constitutes a sentence. Yet some native writers apparently chunk sequences on the basis of meaning rather than syntax, a basis which sometimes violates the conventions of today's graphological sentence. Thus we end in a seemingly paradoxical—and highly frustrating—situation where the writers know but do not know. That is, native-speaker abilities indicate writers know the boundaries of a sentence, but run-ons and comma splices indicate just the opposite.

Treating Run-ons and Comma Splices

Given that run-ons and comma splices today stand a greater chance of evoking not only more negative reaction than in earlier centuries but negative reaction of a much higher degree, and given that unintentional run-ons and comma splices will garner far more negative reaction than intentional ones, what can we do to help students eliminate the unintentional ones? It is unlikely that unintentional run-ons and comma splices will simply disappear if teachers practice benign neglect, especially since students in this age of electronic media tend to do considerably less outside reading on their own. To treat these frequent and highly resistant features, do we, as in the past, simply administer heavier doses of grammar? No, I do not believe this is the easiest or even the most practical solution. If native speakers do, indeed, possess a tacit knowledge of what a sentence is, the logical remedy is not to lay out the principal parts of the sentence in hopes that students will thereby understand the whole. Nor does the remedy lie in the "quick-fix" method of giving a notional, or semantic, definition of a sentence. This approach, as many writing teachers can

attest, quickly deteriorates into defining a burgeoning set of interlinking grammatical terms. Rather, the solution lies in extracting from
students the unconscious knowledge of sentences that they already
possess. By so doing, teachers can not only turn what, at first, seems a
mysterious "gap" in native-speaker abilities into a pedagogical asset
but also demonstrate to themselves and to their students that native
speakers do, in fact, have an underlying knowledge of what constitutes a sentence of their language.

If given a set of genuine (declarative) sentences, native speakers of
English can easily transform them into the corresponding tag and yes-
no questions. For example, if given the (a) sentences below, native
speakers can turn them into the corresponding (b) and (c) sentences.

6. a. Your next-door neighbor is going to sell his car for $400.
   b. Your next-door neighbor is going to sell his car for $400, isn't
      he?
   c. Is your next-door neighbor going to sell his car for $400?
7. a. Nancy, who couldn't wait, ripped open the cellophane
      wrapper on the box.
   b. Nancy, who couldn't wait, ripped open the cellophane
      wrapper on the box, didn't she?
   c. Did Nancy, who couldn't wait, rip open the cellophane
      wrapper on the box?
8. a. For the past six months, Linda and Sue have run five miles
      every day.
   b. For the past six months, Linda and Sue have run five miles
      every day, haven't they?
   c. For the past six months, have Linda and Sue run five miles
      every day?
9. a. Ed and his cousin will buy two tickets each.
   b. Ed and his cousin will buy two tickets each, won't they?
   c. Will Ed and his cousin buy two tickets each?
10. a. You weren't in class for a whole month.
    b. You weren't in class for a whole month, were you?
    c. Weren't you in class for a whole month?

As quick and automatic as this exercise may seem, forming proper tag
and yes-no questions requires knowledge of some complex descriptive rules. For example, yes-no question formation involves a rule
which moves the first auxiliary (i.e., "helping") verb (if there is one)
and the contracted negative -*n't* (if there is one) to the immediate left
of the subject; if there is no first auxiliary verb, the appropriate form of

do (*do, does,* or *did*) is instead added to the immediate left of the subject; if the main verb of the original declarative sentence is *be* (in some dialects, also *have*) and there is no first auxiliary verb, then the main verb *be* (or the main verb *have*) is moved to the immediate left of the subject. Tag-question formation involves knowledge of an even more complex descriptive rule. Roughly stated, if the original declarative sentence is positive, the first auxiliary verb in contracted negative form and the subject in pronominal form are copied in that order to the immediate right of the original declarative sentence; if the original declarative sentence is negative, only the first auxiliary verb and the subject in pronominal form in that order are copied to the immediate right of the original declarative sentence; if there is no first auxiliary verb to copy, then the appropriate form of *do* is added in lieu of the first auxiliary verb to the immediate right of the original sentence; if the main verb of the original declarative sentence is *be* (in some dialects, also *have*) and there is no first auxiliary verb, then the main verb *be* (or the main verb *have*) is copied in lieu of the first auxiliary verb to the immediate right of the original declarative sentence.

Complicated as the yes-no and tag-question rules are, there is no need to teach these two rules formally. Students already have them in their heads. If they did not, they would be unable to produce grammatical tag and yes-no questions in examples 6–10 above or, more tellingly, in everyday conversation. Indeed, because students already possess an unconscious knowledge of these two descriptive rules, they have the capacity to produce an infinite number of grammatical tag and yes-no questions. Even with this prodigious ability, however, they will find it next to impossible to transform the following sequences into their proper and corresponding tag and yes-no questions:

11. Your next-door neighbor is going to sell his car for $400 he should sell it for $800.
12. Nancy, impatient as always, ripped off the cellophane wrapper of the package the icing of the cake came off with it.
13. For the past six months, Linda and Sue have run five miles every day, they really want to win the city championship badly.
14. Ed and his cousin will buy two tickets each, Hank will buy six.
15. You weren't in class for a whole month, it isn't fair.

The reason students cannot transform sequences 11–15 into proper and corresponding tag and yes-no questions lies in the simple fact that the tag and yes-no question rules work only on genuine declarative sentences. Sequences 11 and 12, being run-ons, and sequences 13–15, being comma splices, are nonsentences and, hence, disallow the correct operation of the tag and yes-no question rules. Put more succinctly, tag-question and yes-no question formation operate successfully only on real sentences, not nonsentences. Although students are not consciously aware of this fact, they know it intuitively, as revealed by their inability to produce the proper and corresponding questions from sequences 11–15. If this is so, then students can use their unconscious knowledge of tag and yes-no question formation to help detect and correct run-ons and comma splices. Although either tag-question formation or yes-no question formation will help isolate run-ons and comma splices from genuine sentences, as it will become apparent shortly, using both in combination brings better results.

Two Scenarios

In working with sample sequences like (11–15), teachers can expect two different but related scenarios. In one, students will be unable to transform the run-ons and comma splices into both proper and corresponding tag questions and proper and corresponding yes-no questions. This, of course, is the clearest indication that such sequences are nonsentences of the language. When teachers—and students— reach this assessment, then the stage is set for actually correcting the nonsentence sequences. However, a second and, perhaps, even more revealing scenario may occur. Some students may find that for some nonsentence sequences they cannot form yes-no questions but they can form tag questions. Take, for example, the run-on in (12) above. For this nonsentence sequence, some students may claim, indeed, insist, that the proper and corresponding tag question is (16):

16. *Nancy, impatient as always, ripped off the cellophane wrapper of the package the icing of the cake came off with it, didn't it?

By no means should teachers yield to despair here. Moreover, they should never discourage such incorrect responses; in fact, they should actively solicit them, for such responses, surprisingly, will help students solve the problem of identifying and correcting run-ons and comma splices, not add to it.

Responses such as (16) shed further light on the basic conflict between the conventions of writing and speech, the validity of native-speaker abilities, and, in the end, the value of using both yes-no questions and tag questions as a means of eliminating run-ons and comma splices. The conflict between the conventions of writing and speech, already apparent in the sequence in (12), becomes even more conspicuous in the response in (16), where the graphological sentence comes in conflict with the phonological sentence. Teachers can show this conflict very easily by writing the sequence in (16) on the chalkboard and then having one or two students read it orally at normal (or slightly slower than normal) speed. After having heard the sequence (and, preferably, with their eyes closed), students will notice that one part of the sequence (call it the first part) sounds like a statement, but the remaining, or second part, sounds like a question. While some students may encounter difficulty in detecting run-ons and comma splices in writing, they all, as native speakers of English, should experience no difficulty in distinguishing a question from a nonquestion in speech. More than that, if asked to locate the point where the statement ends and the question begins, they can do so without effort.

Having reached this point with the assistance of their students' unconscious knowledge, teachers can elicit other revealing aspects of sequence 16, again by capitalizing on what students already know as native speakers of English. First the teacher should mark on the chalkboard the separation point between the statement and the question contained in (16) as follows:

17. Nancy, impatient as always, ripped off the cellophane wrapper of the package // the icing of the cake came off with it, didn't it?

Teachers might here question that, though the tag question in (17) seems a proper (i.e., grammatical) one, it does not seem to be a corresponding one; that is, the tag question seems to question not all of sequence 17 but only the part to the right of the double slash (//). To raise further doubts that sequence 17 really consists of two sentences rather than one, teachers should ask students to transform the statement part of the sequence (i.e., the first part) into a tag question and a yes-no question, a task which should yield, *Nancy, impatient as always, ripped off the cellophane wrapper of the package, didn't she?* and *Did Nancy, impatient as always, rip off the cellophane wrapper of the package?* To verify that the second part of (17) is also a sentence, teachers can ask students to provide the yes-no question counterpart (*Did the icing of the cake come off with it?*). After having accomplished these tasks—tasks which come easily because they rely on linguistic knowledge that native speakers already possess—students come to see more clearly not only why sequences like (16) actually consist of misjoined sentences but also precisely where the misjoining occurs.

More Complex Cases

Run-ons or comma splices consisting of three or more misjoined sentences can be handled in a similar fashion. Consider, for example, the comma splice in (18):

18. The Minnesota Twins won the World Series in 1987, then the Los Angeles Dodgers won in 1988, now the Oakland Athletics have won it.

With a three-sentence comma splice like (18), teachers should again try to elicit from students the corresponding tag question. The tag-question rule either will not work (a strong indication of nonsentence-hood), or it will apply only to the last sentence in the comma splice (i.e., *The Minnesota Twins won the World Series in 1987, then the Los Angeles Dodgers won in 1988, now the Oakland Athletics have won it, haven't they?*). If students are asked to read this whole tag-question sequence aloud, they can again separate it into a question part and a statement part. If students are asked to explain where the *they* and, particularly, the *have* in *haven't they* come from, they will see that the source sentence of the tag question is not the whole sequence in (18) but only *now the Oakland Athletics have won it.* (Teachers can ask students to apply the yes-no question rule to *now the Oakland Athletics have won it* for further verification of sentencehood.) Having convinced themselves that *now the Oakland Athletics have won it* is a separate sentence, students should be asked to form a tag question from the remaining part (i.e., *The Minnesota Twins won the World Series in 1987, then the Los Angeles Dodgers won in 1988*). At this point, instructors can utilize the strategies suggested for the two-sentence comma splices above. The overall strategy for handling run-ons and comma splices with more than two constituent sentences is working from right to left, eliminating, one by one, the rightmost sentence by applying the tag-question rule. The yes-no question rule can be used as verification for each sentence that the tag-question rule isolates.

In teaching the above method for identifying run-ons and comma splices, teachers should keep in mind that the competing semantically based system of punctuation continually seeks to reassert itself. The competing system becomes especially apparent in cases like (19) and (20) below, which exemplify a comma splice and, for some students, one resulting and highly likely (but noncorresponding) tag question:

19. Bill isn't going to the dance, Mary isn't going to the dance either.
20. *Bill isn't going to the dance, Mary isn't going to the dance either, are they?

The presence and effect of the semantically based system of punctuation is manifested not only in the writing of the comma splice itself in (19) but also in the appearance of the pronoun *they* (instead of the more expected *she*) in the tag of (20). Because the meaning bond is particularly strong in short parallel sentences, students will often not only misjoin the sentences in writing but also compound the subjects of the individual sentences when applying the tag-question rule. When dealing with such cases, teachers can exploit native-speaker knowledge to demonstrate that (20) cannot be the corresponding tag question to (19). Teachers can ask students what the *they* refers to (or "stands for"). Given the tight semantic bond here, students who claim that (20) is the corresponding tag question to (19) will say "Bill and Mary." Yet, "Bill and Mary" can be the correct answer only if the original sentence is *Bill and Mary aren't going to the dance* (which is not the case). Students will readily agree if they are asked to form the corresponding tag question for this sentence. In brief, since *Bill and Mary aren't going to the dance* is not the original sentence, the tag question in (20) cannot be the corresponding tag question for (19). However, responses like (20) are still highly useful since they split a comma splice or run-on into a statement and a question.

Advantages of the Approach

Having its basis in already-acquired linguistic knowledge, the method sketched above provides a more inductive and more easily accessible means of detecting run-ons and comma splices than traditional methods. Although students often forget (or inadequately learn) abstract and vague definitions of "sentence" or "independent clause" and the parts of a sentence, they do not forget (or inadequately learn) how to form tag and yes-no questions. By requiring students to use what they already know, this method exploits and makes more tangible not only their tacit knowledge of the tag- and yes-no question rules but also their tacit knowledge of sentence boundaries, boundaries which unskilled writers sometimes fail to signal in writing, as is conventionally required and expected. Tacit knowledge of the tag-question and yes-no question rules helps students identify these boundary violations. Neither of these two question rules work when applied to run-ons and comma splices (providing strong evidence that the source sequences are not genuine sentences). Alternatively, only one of them (i.e., the tag-question rule) will work, but only because student judgments here are more in tune with native intuitions of sentence boundaries than with the incorrectly marked boundaries of run-ons and comma splices.

The formation of a proper but noncorresponding tag question from a run-on or comma splice represents a good example of knowledge disguised as error. (When dealing with run-ons and comma splices, teachers should, by whatever means possible, encourage, even "force" such helpful errors if they do not come readily or voluntarily.) By forming a proper but noncorresponding tag question from a run-on or comma splice, students inadvertently (but correctly) split the run-on or comma splice into its component sentences. This split occurs not because students' knowledge of the tag-question rule is lacking or defective but rather because that knowledge is accurate and secure. When applying (or when forced to apply) the tag-question rule to nonsentence sequences, students will unconsciously (and correctly) apply the rule only to structures which allow it, namely, genuine sentences. That students can thus split run-ons and comma splices into component sentences indirectly reveals their tacit and linguistically correct knowledge.

Besides revealing students' underlying knowledge of the tag-question rule, the inadvertent splitting of run-ons and comma splices into component sentences brings therapeutic benefits. For one, it makes perception of the misjoined independent clauses much easier. By turning the last independent clause of the sequence into a tag question, the run-on or comma splice is changed from a sequence of statement plus statement to a sequence of statement plus question. This conversion facilitates the identification of the component sentences because, generally, separating two unlikes is easier than separating two likes (compare the task of separating reds from blues to that of separating shades of blue). Besides indicating that run-ons and comma splices consist of more than one sentence, splitting them presents a golden opportunity for students to test their judgments of what constitutes a sentence. By applying the tag- and yes-no question rules to the component sentences, students can verify the validity of their judgments. As students perform these verification tests on the component sentences of run-ons and comma splices, they will, with the aid of their teachers, come to see that both tag-question formation and yes-no question formation explicitly mark sentence boundaries. Tag-question formation marks the right boundary by placing a tag (e.g., *didn't she, shouldn't he, won't they*) to the immediate right of the sentence. Yes-no question formation marks the left boundary by placing the moved auxiliary verb (or the added *do* form) at the beginning of the sentence.

Some Practical Benefits

Although the approach described above may not work for all students (e.g., students in the lower primary grades or non-native students who lack fluency in English), it can potentially work for all others. If native writers know how to form tag and yes-no questions—which they should as native speakers of the language—they possess an easily accessible and always available means of checking for run-ons and comma splices without first having to undergo formal instruction in grammar. They simply use what they already know. For teachers, this means less time and effort spent on formal grammar instruction and more time and energy to devote to other and more important aspects of writing. Although unconventional features such as run-ons and comma splices require attention at some stage in the writing process (preferably during the rewriting or proofreading stages), teachers should bear in mind that treatment of such errors should comprise neither the principal activities of a writing program nor its principal goal.

For students, the benefits can be no less significant. First, the proposed approach relieves students from many hours of difficult and often tedious lessons in grammar where rote memorization seems more important than principles. The approach proposed here not only greatly shortens the time allotted to formal grammar study but offers a more interactive and, I believe, a more interesting way to learn about grammar. Because traditional approaches to grammar have generally failed to build on underlying linguistic abilities, teachers have not only made their task more difficult and time-consuming but also alienated a large number of students who might otherwise pursue grammar study with greater enthusiasm. Second, the proposed approach enables students to learn more about their remarkable abilities as native speakers of the language. By generating their own language data, forming hypotheses, and testing them with their native-speaker intuitions of the language, students come to learn more not only about language and inductive reasoning but also about themselves—of what it means to possess knowledge *of* a language rather than possessing knowledge *about* a language. Finally, the proposed approach promotes greater self-confidence and self-reliance. Instead of ignoring underlying linguistic abilities or viewing such abilities negatively (i.e., as a lack or defect in such abilities), the proposed approach enables students to demonstrate and verify for themselves the prodigious and often untapped linguistic abilities they bring to the classroom every day.

5 Fragments and Beyond

In daily speech, sentence fragments abound. Whether we notice them or not, admit them or not, we speak with fragments constantly in conversation. Yet, in formal writing, fragments occupy a more restricted status, at times begrudgingly accepted, often severely criticized. Like run-ons and comma splices, they fail to uphold—or rather fail to consummate—sentence boundaries. Like run-ons and comma splices, fragments illustrate the conflict between speech and writing. This conflict, however, reveals much about what native writers already know about both the syntactic and informational structure of the sentence. This chapter discusses the status of fragments, their causes, and their remedy. More important, the discussion will show that fragments, far from indicating a linguistic defect, offer a promising means for students to learn more deeply about how not only sentences but also whole texts are put together.

Fragments in Speech

That fragments tend to proliferate in writing comes as no surprise if we consider the status of fragments in conversation. Take, for example, this series of speech exchanges between Speaker A and Speaker B from Wardhaugh's *How Conversation Works* (1985, 193-94):

> A: (Walks to kitchen) Been home long?
> B: Just a few minutes. I was out in a school all afternoon.
> A: Ah! We eating at home?
> B: Could, I suppose.
> A: No. Let's go out. I've got to look for a book.
> B: OK. Give me a few minutes to get changed. By the way . . .
> A: Yes?
> B: Oh, nothing. Chinese food?
> A: Yeah. If you want. I'll take the dog out for a walk while you get ready. (Loudly) Rufus!

As everyday conversations go, this naturally occurring example is typical in its mundaneness—and its use of sentence fragments. If we include the *yes* or *no* responses (or their variants) as fragments, we find that at least one fragment occurs in every speaking turn between A and B. Though frequently condemned in writing, fragments are not only accepted but expected in everyday conversation. If we turned every fragment in the conversational sequence above into its probable and corresponding sentence, the speakers would sound extremely formal—as if they were "talking prose." With fragments being so common in everyday speech, most researchers consider the basic unit of conversation to be not the sentence but the utterance, a unit which subsumes both fragments and sentences and their combinations.

Fragments in Writing

Why fragments occur with greater frequency in speech than in writing has, of course, to do with the differing conventions between the two media. However, a more enlightening explanation for the greater frequency comes from some stark differences in the communicative situation between speech and writing. It is these differences which permit, indeed facilitate, the greater use of fragments in speech. Because speech (in contrast to writing) typically involves face-to-face interaction, participants can augment and enhance messages not only with features peculiar to speech (e.g., intonation, pitch) but also with nonverbal resources such as eye gaze and bodily gestures. Abetted by these extra resources, truncated messages have a greater chance of being communicated. Also, because of the frequent changes in speaking turns in conversation and the relative shortness of turns (both exemplified in the conversation above), participants find it easier to hold in memory and to build on the assumptions established by prior speech. That is, because speakers in face-to-face conversation can create and take advantage of shared assumptions quickly, they can, without loss of content, shorten their utterances (i.e., speak with fragments). Because of the slowness of the writing process, writers often cannot make such assumptions of shared knowledge. Finally, if misunderstandings occur, speakers have access to immediate feedback to clarify or make a quick repair of the unsuccessful utterance. Put in another way, fragments in conversational situations generally entail less risk than they do in writing because repair mechanisms can be more quickly implemented. Because of differences in the communicative situations of the two media, speakers, in contrast to writers, can more easily abbreviate their utterances; hence, the greater permissibility and frequency of fragments in speech.

With the increased influence of the spoken medium on the written medium, fragments now seem to crop up more frequently in writing, even formal writing. Connors and Lunsford, in their study of error frequency (1988, 403), found 1,217 instances of fragments in 3,000 college themes, or 4.2 percent of the total formal errors found, a percentage high enough to make fragments the twelfth most frequently occurring formal error in the study. A clearer link between oral culture and the increased number of fragments in writing comes from Sloan's (1979) study, in which 1,000 freshman themes written between 1973 and 1976 were compared with a like number of themes written between 1950 and 1957. In addition to finding a higher incidence of such words as *thing, interesting, great, amazing,* and other "diffusive words" of oral discourse, Sloan found in the 1973–76 themes a growing unfamiliarity with the written word as indicated by significant increases in the following: run-together words (e.g., *alot, noone*), confusion of similar sounding words (e.g., *their/there, to/too, effect/affect*), misspellings, omission of the verb ending *-ed*, proliferation of the second-person *you*, comma faults, and last but not least, sentence fragments. According to Sloan (158), the number of fragments in the 1970s themes surpassed those in the 1950s themes by a ratio of 1,847/638, or roughly 3:1. (The analogous ratio with comma splices, incidentally, was 2,327/588, or about 4:1.) Although some may question if all of Sloan's features are exclusive markers of oral culture, the aggregate does suggest an increased and probably pervasive influence of today's oral culture on writing.

The Positive Side of Fragments

Although those who have invested many years punctiliously learning the conventions of writing may condemn the onslaught of oral culture on writing, this onslaught may not be as pernicious as the cognoscenti believe. Robin Lakoff (1982) makes clear the advantages and disadvantages of the spontaneity of oral discourse and the forethought of written discourse:

> As spontaneity and forethought have their advantages, they have equally inalienable disadvantages. Truly spontaneous discourse has an immediacy, and emotional directness, that is truly exhilarating; at the same time, it carries the burden of immediacy: lack of

> clarity, use of the wrong word or phrase, hesitation, repetition, and so on. These are necessary concomitants of true spontaneity: we cannot be spontaneous and polished at once. Planned discourse avoids these pitfalls; but at the same time, it necessarily lacks warmth, closeness, and vividness. (242)

While we should not ignore the disadvantages of fragments in formal writing, we should certainly acknowledge their advantages. Fragments, being a part of the spontaneity of oral discourse, without question contribute a sense of immediacy and directness to what otherwise might be cold and stuffy prose. When employed skillfully, fragments can also convey questions (*Me worry?*) or commands (*Stop!*) or exclamations (*What a party!*), emphasize ideas, reduce excessive complexity, and even serve as transitions (*Now for the sad part*). Indeed, because of the sentence-like functions many fragments play in writing, Kline and Memering (1977) refer to such fragments by the more descriptive and less pejorative term "independent minor sentences." In a less pejorative light also, certain fragments appear to be early attempts at some late-blooming syntactic structures. Harris (1981) points out that the vast majority of the fragments she finds in her students' writing are segments that have been separated from a preceding or following main clause—what Kline and Memering might classify as "dependent minor sentences" (i.e., fragments which do not function as independent sentences but are tied syntactically and semantically to an adjacent sentence). Harris claims that such fragments are probably early but mispunctuated occurrences of Christensen's final free modifiers, a type of syntactic construction found in mature writers (176–77).

Also on the bright side—and also in keeping with one of the central themes of this study—fragments reveal more of the unconscious and prodigious linguistic abilities of native speakers. Language has been described by many as a "window to the mind." To the extent of its truth, this metaphor gives powerful impetus to the study of the relationship between language and mind. Unfortunately, some have interpreted the metaphor too literally, resulting in unfavorable and inaccurate characterizations of students who happen to write (or speak) with fragments. Such students are sometimes viewed as possessing not just a defective language but, to carry through with the window metaphor, also a defective mind, one lacking in logic or coherence or both. Yet just as complete sentences do not necessarily reflect a wholly rational and coherent mind, so fragments do not necessarily reflect a fragmented and incoherent one.

Recognizing the Structure of Fragments

Certainly fragments ought not to be thrown into one grab bag labeled
"defective sentences." Although some fragments may be incomplete
as far as sentences go, they reveal well-formedness in other ways. For
example, although students who understand the basics of end
punctuation may write fragments such as those in the (a) examples
below, it is highly improbable that they will write fragments such as
those in the (b) examples:

1. a. Sam ended up cleaning up his room. Which he doesn't like.
   b. Sam ended up cleaning up his room which he. Doesn't like.
2. a. The soldiers marched straight ahead. Into an ambush.
   b. The soldiers marched straight ahead into. An ambush.
3. a. Arthur missed an easy surprise quiz. Because he skipped class.
   b. Arthur missed an easy surprise quiz because. He skipped
      class.
4. a. It soon became very obvious. That the train wasn't going to
      Chicago.
   b. It soon became very obvious that the train. Wasn't going to
      Chicago.

Despite the fragments (or, really, because of them), examples such as
(1–4) reveal that students who are native speakers of English and who
write with unconventional breaks in sentences nonetheless form
fragments out of well-established syntactic units. For example, in (1a),
the break is made precisely at the onset of the relative clause *which he
doesn't like*; in (2a), the break is made precisely at the onset of the
prepositional phrase *into an ambush*. In (3a), the break occurs precisely
at the boundary of a subordinate clause, and in (4a), precisely at the
boundary of a complement clause.

    Furthermore, students who write with fragments are aware of what
makes a well-formed fragment not only in terms of the preceding
syntactic unit but also in terms of the fragment itself. That is, while
students may write fragments like those in the (a) examples below,
they will not write fragments such as those in the (b) examples:

5. a. That used to be my favorite hobby. Making paper airplanes.
   b. That used to be my favorite hobby. *Airplanes paper making.
6. a. When you invite the guests. Make sure not to invite my
      brother.
   b. When you invite the guests. *Sure make not invite to my brother.

In other words, fragments themselves have internal structure which students readily recognize. Furthermore, in accordance with Morgan's (1973) study, "Sentence Fragments and the Notion 'Sentence,'" fragments have other sentence-like properties, which all native students (but not all non-native ones) will recognize readily or, at least, recognize if pointed out to them. Like sentences, fragments can be structurally ambiguous, as in (7), and capable of potentially infinite embedding, as in (8):

7. What does Eloise hate? Boring people. (i.e., 'Eloise hates people who are boring' or 'Eloise hates to bore people')

8. Started by a man who worked in a glass factory, which was located in a small town, which was founded in 1881, which . . . .

Fragments can also exhibit synonymy, which native students, again, will recognize, as in (9) and (10):

9. What's so funny? Mervin being chased up a tree by the dog.

10. What's so funny? The dog chasing Mervin up a tree.

Thus, while fragments at first seem to indicate an imperfect knowledge of the language, they, in fact, serve as evidence of just the opposite. Far from being linguistically deficient, native students who write with fragments already know a great deal about the boundaries and internal structure of fragments, regardless of whether these segments are relative clauses, prepositional phrases, subordinate clauses, complement clauses, and the like. This tacit knowledge includes not just syntactic properties but also semantic ones, for these same students have also acquired the ability to recognize ambiguity and synonymy in fragments.

Yet do students who have knowledge of the parts also have knowledge of the whole? Granted that students who write with fragments know something about fragments, but do they know what constitutes a genuine sentence? The answer here can only be affirmative. While fragments may be incomplete sentences, they do not in any way reflect incomplete knowledge of sentences. Native students who write frequently with fragments know what a genuine sentence is as much as those native students who rarely or never write with fragments. That is, the underlying linguistic knowledge of both types of students is the same: they both know what constitutes a sentence of their language. If unintentional fragments do occur, they are errors of linguistic performance, not of linguistic competence.

Verifying the Underlying Knowledge of Sentences

To bring to the surface the unconscious and underlying knowledge of a sentence, all teachers need to do is ask students to form corresponding tag and yes-no questions from any sequence of words. For sequences like (11-14), students will easily convert the declarative sentences in (a) to the tag questions in (b) and the yes-no questions in (c).

11. a. The boy who lives across the street can swim well.
    b. The boy who lives across the street can swim well, can't he?
    c. Can the boy who lives across the street swim well?

12. a. Our school was built in 1907 by money obtained from a lottery.
    b. Our school was built in 1907 by money obtained from a lottery, wasn't it?
    c. Was our school built in 1907 by money obtained from a lottery?

13. a. Our teacher said she danced the jitterbug when she was young.
    b. Our teacher said she danced the jitterbug when she was young, didn't she?
    c. Did our teacher say she danced the jitterbug when she was young?

14. a. Many people nowadays won't give up their seats to senior citizens.
    b. Many people nowadays won't give up their seats to senior citizens, will they?
    c. Won't many people nowadays give up their seats to senior citizens?

While students will find no difficulty in transforming the sequences in (11-14) to the corresponding tag and yes-no questions, they will encounter immense difficulty in doing so with the sequences in (15-19):

15. From the store which sells flashlights and camping equipment.

16. Whatever you want to do next week.

17. His lifelong dream of playing shortstop for the New York Yankees.

18. When my mom didn't answer the phone right away.

19. For instance, my chewing gum during class.

The reason students cannot transform the sequences in (15-19) to corresponding tag and yes-no questions stems from a simple but pedagogically valuable fact: tag-question and yes-no question formation work only on genuine sentences, not on fragments (which, by definition, are not sentences). Although students may not be consciously aware of this fact, let alone express it until teachers reveal it to them, they must already have tacit knowledge of it. How else can we plausibly explain why native-English students so unreflectingly and profusely form tag and yes-no questions from sequences like (11-14) in daily speech, yet rarely if ever attempt to form tag or yes-no questions from sequences like (15-19)? The most plausible answer seems to be that students already know (unconsciously) that they can't. And the reason they can't is that such sequences are not sentences. Put in a nutshell, students give evidence of their unconscious knowledge of what constitutes a genuine sentence by their ability to transform sentences like (11-14) and also by their inability to transform fragments like (15-19). For teachers of writing, this is a boon. If native writers can form corresponding tag and yes-no questions, as they demonstrate each day in conversation, and if they are made aware of how this ability interacts positively with genuine sentences and negatively with sentence fragments, then native writers—particularly, those experiencing problems with unintentional fragments—possess a ready means of checking the sentencehood of any sequence they write.[1]

Applying the Underlying Knowledge

Teachers can exploit what students already know about sentences— and particularly, fragments—in even more fruitful ways. In the ensuing discussion, I will suggest how the knowledge underlying the formation and use of fragments can form the basis for clarifying and unifying a host of seemingly disparate writing problems, not only sentence-level ones but also some that go beyond the borders of the sentence. In the process, the discussion will necessarily turn from a syntactic perspective, as has been the case thus far, to a more semantic/pragmatic one. The rationale for this change in perspective is essentially threefold: (1) to illustrate how a semantic/pragmatic perspective can prove beneficial in addressing many persistent problems traditionally treated with syntactic approaches, (2) to show further the value of exploiting what students already know about language and, more generally, (3) to suggest why the study of grammar, as it is presently conceived and presented, requires a different orientation if it is to make a more productive contribution to writing improvement. This different orientation will not solve all writing problems—no one approach can—but it will give teachers a more unified basis for tackling many diverse kinds of problems found in student writing.

Given and New Information

As made clear by discourse analysts such as Daneš, Firbas, Clark and Haviland, and Chafe, information in sentences of coherent texts is not arranged randomly. More specifically, information is separated into "given" and "new" information, with each typically parceled out to certain parts of the sentence. Given (i.e., old or deducible) information is information that has been mentioned previously or is otherwise assumed to be common or shared between addresser and addressee (here, writer and reader, respectively). It is shared because of mutual knowledge of the cultural context (e.g., knowledge of what *the sun, the Constitution,* or *the Civil War* specifically refers to), the communicative context (e.g., knowledge of who *I* or *you* or *the writer* or *the reader* specifically refers to), or the textual context (e.g., knowledge of what *the latter sentence* and *the former sentence* or *the idea just mentioned* specifically refers to). In brief, given information is information that can be recovered from the context, either linguistic or extralinguistic. New information, on the other hand, is not common or shared between addresser and addressee. It is information which is not recoverable from the linguistic or extralinguistic context.

Customarily, texts in English present both given and new information as readers move linearly from left to right. For example, in the first sentence of the two-sentence sequence *The man whom we all know died. His death came suddenly,* the noun phrase *The man whom we all know* may be considered given information and *died* new information; in the second sentence, *His death* represents given information, and *came suddenly,* new information. Although the very first sentence of a text may contain all new (or, at least, all new textual) information, subsequent sentences will probably have a combination of both given and new information. A combination of given and new ensures that the information presented will be not completely redundant (all given information) or completely incoherent (all new information). What is new information, once mentioned, becomes given information. Given information remains given until it disappears from immediate (or "short-term") memory, whereupon it must be reestablished, or "reactivated," as given information.

Especially pertinent for our purposes is the linear arrangement, or organization, of given and new information in individual sentences. In most declarative sentences, given information occurs at or near the beginning of the sentence, and new information at or near the end. This arrangement of information seems, in general, to coincide with the traditional subject and predicate of the sentence, respectively. However, just as a subject noun phrase (i.e., the "complete subject") and a verb phrase (i.e., the predicate) both exhibit a core and peripheral elements, so too do given and new information. As Firbas (1986, 51–54) suggests, both given and new information normally have a peak, or core, in the sentence, with the peripheral elements serving as transition to the peak. With given information, the peak tends to occur more towards the left boundary of the sentence; with new information, the peak tends to occur more towards the right boundary. For example, in a sequence of subject plus verb plus adverb, the new information conveyed in the predicate (here, verb plus adverb) would tend to reach its peak in the adverb since this element lies nearest the end of the sentence. In a sequence of subject plus verb plus direct object, the new information would tend to reach its peak in the direct object, since it lies nearest the end of the sentence. The informational structure—and its syntactic correlates—can be seen in the subject plus verb plus direct object sentences in (20) and (21):

20. The boy picked up a stone.

21. He caused a major fire.

In (20), the given information is *The boy* (as indicated by the occurrence of the definite article *The*, which presumes shared knowledge), and the new information is *picked up a stone*, with *a stone* being the peak. In (21), the given information is *He* (since pronouns presume prior mention or knowledge of an antecedent), and the new information is *caused a major fire*, with *a major fire* being the peak. As evident in both (20) and (21), both given and new information can be signaled not only implicitly by sentence position but also overtly by grammatical elements, for example, pronouns and definite articles for given information, indefinite articles for new information. In (20) and (21) both these devices are in alignment. We see better the interactive nature of sentence position and grammatical elements by misaligning the two as in (22) and (23):

22. A boy picked up the stone.

23. A major fire was caused by him.

In (22), the given information (*the stone*) occurs at the end of the sentence and the new information (*A boy*) at the beginning. Although the given and new information is misaligned with position, the sentence is still interpretable. However, the reader is forced to construct a less natural context to interpret the sentence, for example, one in which a known stone is picked up by an unknown boy who enters upon the scene. Put more schematically, a "given" object (the stone) is acted upon by a "new" agent (a boy), who enters upon the scene and performs a "new" act of picking up. In such a context, the sentence makes sense, but the reader must, of course, do some extra work. In (23), the given and new information are again misaligned, with the given information (*him*) at the end and the new information at the beginning. Although syntactically impeccable, (23) seems pragmatically unnatural unless contrastive stress is placed on *him* to indicate that the causer of the fire was a particular male person and not some other person. That is, the sentence means something like 'I assert that it was him who caused a major fire and not someone else.' The contrastive stress on *him*, in effect, makes *him* new information, and thereby puts new information at the end of the sentence. It is worth stressing that the oddness of (23) stems not from the mere use of the passive (as many teachers are inclined to say) but from the misalignment of the given and new information which passivization creates here. In contrast, the active counterpart of (23)—that is, *He caused a major fire*—sounds more natural, not because it is nonpassive but rather because the given and new information are in correct alignment with sentence position. In brief, the problem with the readability of (23) is principally semantic/pragmatic rather than syntactic.

Even though the short discussion above hardly does justice to the complexities of the organization of information in sentences, it is important to realize that native writers already have the basis for recognizing the distinction between given and new information and, just as important, utilizing that distinction in written discourse. Indeed, they frequently and unconsciously demonstrate this knowledge every day in the fragments they produce in speech (and in writing). If teachers have ever asked students the following kinds of elliptical questions and received the following kinds of elliptical responses, they will readily attest to this kind of unconscious knowledge:

Teacher: And what city do the Yankees play in?
Student: In New York. (= The Yankees play in New York City.)

Teacher: And the Dodgers? (= And what city do the Dodgers play in?)

Student: Los Angeles. (= The Dodgers play in Los Angeles.)

If students did not already possess the knowledge of what constitutes given and new information, they would be unable to produce the appropriate fragments as responses (let alone understand the teacher's second question) in the exchange above. In compliance with the teacher's requests for information, the fragment answers here present new information with the given information deleted. To form and use such fragments as responses, however, the student must first know the difference between given and new information; otherwise, it would be difficult to explain why certain kinds of information are deleted in fragment responses and certain kinds are not. In other words, fragments, despite their tenuous status in formal written discourse, reflect valuable, already-acquired yet tacit knowledge of the information structure of sentences. If so, fragments, rather than being merely defects to be condemned, can serve as resources to help identify the given-and-new information structure of sentences.

Clarifying Some Common Stylistic Errors

Pronoun Reference

Before going into further details of the given-and-new information structure, it is worth pointing out that, besides clarifying an appropriate use of passive sentences, the given-new concept provides a more unified basis for clarifying a wide range of frequent and seemingly disparate kinds of writing problems traditionally labeled as "formal," or "stylistic," errors. One obvious area concerns vague pronoun reference. Vague pronoun reference occurs not because writers do not know the principles of pronominal substitution but rather because they sometimes fail to establish the antecedent of pronouns as given information. Although such writers correctly substitute pronouns for the antecedents, they assume the establishment of antecedence where the majority of readers do not. This misjudgment of given information involves not only cases in which writers neglect altogether to mention the antecedent of the pronoun (e.g., *It's crazy*) but also cases in which writers, after the first mention of an antecedent, fail to maintain unambiguous reference (e.g., *Judy finally paid Sally ten dollars, but she said it was too much*). So general and widespread is vague pronoun reference that Connors and Lunsford (1988, 403) list it as the second most frequently occurring error in the essays that they examined. The given-new concept offers one useful way of clarifying the causes of this writing problem.

Restrictive and Nonrestrictive Clauses

Less obvious, but just as pertinent to the given-new concept, is the distinction between restrictive and nonrestrictive relative clauses. Restrictive and nonrestrictive relative clauses are similar syntactically insofar as they both have a characteristic form and occur after nouns (more correctly, after noun phrases and pronouns); however, they differ semantically in that restrictive relative clauses (as in *The car which Alice rented needs a new muffler*) limit, or "restrict," the range of the meaning of the head noun, whereas nonrestrictive relative clauses (as in *The car, which Alice rented, needs a new muffler*) merely add extra or nonessential information. But restrictive and nonrestrictive relative clauses also exhibit a fundamental difference with respect to given and new information. Restrictive relative clauses assume shared knowledge on the part of the writer and reader of a set of items, out of which the restrictive relative clause specifies or picks out a certain subset. That is, what restrictive relative clauses do is to bring into prominence a specific member of a previously established (or contextually deducible) set. In contrast, nonrestrictive relative clauses do not bring into prominence any specific member from a previously established set. Although native speakers signal these distinctions in conversation by intonation and pauses, writers unfamiliar with the conventions of punctuation often fail to make the distinction in print. (The Connors-Lunsford study ranks the mispunctuation of nonrestrictive and restrictive elements fifth and seventeenth, respectively, in their "top twenty" formal error list.) Again, the given-new concept can help clarify the nature of the problem.

Other Kinds of Stylistic Errors

Other kinds of stylistic errors which can be usefully viewed with respect to the given-new distinction include the following (I have given the Connors-Lunsford ranking in parentheses where applicable):

> *Tense shift* (10): time of the event or events indicated by tense not established as given

Unnecessary shift in person (11): person or persons referred to not established as given

Subject-verb agreement (14): e.g., collective nouns; reader and writer disagree whether the subject acts as a group or individually: *The committee argue constantly* vs. *The committee acts in unison*

Incorrect use of definite and indefinite articles: *the* presupposes given information; *a/an* presuppose new information

Incorrect semicolon usage: joined clauses not established as closely connected: *The Detroit Pistons won the NBA Championship in 1989; the Los Angeles Lakers won it in 1988* vs. *Helen loves fast foods; the Los Angeles Lakers won the NBA Championship in 1988*

Although an error of a slightly different nature, the lack of necessary quotation marks and/or proper documentation in research writing also involves the given-new distinction since the lapse involves a disagreement between writer and reader on what is public (i.e., given) knowledge and nonpublic (i.e., new) knowledge.

It is, of course, easy to trivialize the given-new distinction by arguing that all and everything in the universe divides into given and new information and, thus, the distinction is simply too crude to employ in writing instruction. Yet, while the given-new distinction is an expansive one, the scope of the two categories can be narrowed by focusing only on information relevant to the text in question (e.g., on information which should but does not actually appear in the text). Furthermore, Prague School linguists, such as Firbas and Daneš, have identified finer distinctions within the overarching given-new distinction. While these distinctions are unnecessary for the general discussion here, they include, among others, "theme" (what the sentence is about) versus "rheme" (what is said about the theme), "hypertheme" (a superordinate, or encompassing, theme) versus "subtheme" (a subordinate theme associated with and derived from a hypertheme). Each of these categories is further delineated by the degree of "communicative dynamism," which measures the strength of communicative import of the information conveyed. Prince (1981), in her taxonomy of given and new information, divides new information into "brand new" information (information which the addresser assumes is unknown in any way to the addressee) and "unused" information (information which the addresser assumes is known to the addressee as part of background knowledge but which is not currently in the addressee's consciousness). What we have been calling "given" information, Prince divides into "inferrable" information (information deducible from already mentioned information) and "evoked" information (either "situationally evoked" information, that is, information saliently present in the discourse context, or "textually evoked" information, information saliently present in the preceding text). It is also possible to refine (and describe) the analysis of given and new information by bringing in, as Givón (1989, 214-35) suggests, such influencing factors as the degree of importance and degree of predictability of the two basic categories. Furthermore, though the basic categories of given and new are expansive, it is this very expansiveness which, in the end, provides a unified way of capturing what is common to many diverse kinds of syntactic, semantic, and graphological writing problems. The common element is usually the lack of some relevant information to be established as given in the text. In this connection, it cannot be stressed enough that the medium of writing not only requires the establishment of relevant given information but requires it more quickly, more frequently, and more overtly than does the medium of speech. It goes without saying that the more expeditiously and skillfully teachers make this need clear and the more expeditiously and skillfully writers fulfill this need, the more transparent and effective the writing. As suggested by the discussion above, writing problems often involve information which writers already possess but fail to manifest in the form of given information (i.e, as shared information). As such, these writing problems exemplify once more the general theme that, in many instances, writers not so much lack the requisite knowledge to solve writing problems but fail either to use that knowledge or, as in the case of given and new information, to make that knowledge overt in print.

Vocabulary

It is worth mentioning that the given-new distinction also helps unify and clarify a vast range of vocabulary errors, or what is often called "wrong word" choices (which rank fourth in the Connors-Lunsford "top twenty" list). Put in terms of the given-new distinction, vocabulary errors involve instances in which the writer and reader do not agree either on the word meanings themselves (i.e., unshared word meanings) or on the utilization of word meanings in a particular context (i.e., shared word meanings but unshared social use). The first case can be illustrated with the use of the noun *bachelor*, as in (24); the second case, with the use of the verb *croak*, as in (25):

24. My sister's a bachelor, too, since she's unmarried.

25. I am very sorry to hear that your father passed away. When did he croak?

While it is clear that the infelicity in (24) arises from a lack of shared knowledge of the meaning of a specific word (i.e., *bachelor*), it is plausible to argue that the infelicity in (25) also arises from a lack of shared knowledge between writer and reader (or speaker and hearer). In (25), the writer (or speaker) conveys in the first sentence not only his or her knowledge about the death of the addressee's father but also a sympathetic and respectful attitude towards that death. What is conveyed (i.e., established as given or shared) in the first sentence of (25), however, clashes with the choice of the word *croak* in the second sentence. That is to say, the background (i.e., given) information created by the first sentence now seems unshared by writer and audience; hence, the incongruity and oddity of the second sentence. In essence, (25) shows that writers establish shared, or background, information with respect not only to word meanings but also to contexts. Put in slightly different terms, writers create and then place in the background or the foreground not just meanings but also contexts.

Clarifying Emphasis and Coherence

The given-new concept probably finds its greatest utility in clarifying and unifying two highly neglected and highly frustrating writing problems of a broader scope, namely, lack of emphasis and coherence. Because writing lacking emphasis and coherence usually exhibits no traces of overt "grammatical errors," both students and teachers find the source of the problem difficult to pinpoint, much less treat.

Emphasis

Consider first writing that lacks proper emphasis, or prominence. Because teachers usually receive very little exposure to emphasis in their formal training, they teach very little about it in the classroom. As a consequence, students often end up equating emphasis with its closest counterpart in speech, namely, contrastive stress. Hence, what is expressed louder in speech gets expressed "louder" in writing— with single or multiple underlinings, single or multiple exclamation points, capital letters, or sometimes a combination of all three. Yet ideas in writing can be given prominence more subtly and usually more effectively by syntactic means. For example, it is well known that some late-blooming syntactic constructions can give prominence to ideas. These constructions usually involve complex focusing transformations like *It*-Cleft (e.g., *It was lightning which started a major forest fire in Yellowstone in 1988*), *What*-Cleft (e.g., *What started a major forest fire in Yellowstone in 1988 was lightning*), and Passive (e.g., *A major forest fire was started in Yellowstone in 1988 by lightning*). While such constructions are undoubtedly useful in highlighting ideas, they do not always fit the occasion, nor are all students (particularly those in the lower grades) comfortable in using them, since these constructions tend to be less established in speech. Teachers can, however, provide students with a more fundamental and, in many ways, a more versatile method of giving prominence to ideas—by rearranging ideas in the base sentence. Consider the following syntactic variants in (26):

26. a. Lightning started a major forest fire in 1988 in Yellowstone.
    b. Lightning started a major forest fire in Yellowstone in 1988.
    c. In Yellowstone in 1988, lightning started a major forest fire.

Although the three sentences in (26) all express the same cognitive meaning (i.e., lightning did the starting; a major forest fire was what was started; the event took place in Yellowstone in the year 1988), the three sentences do not all have the same emphasis. In (26a), the emphasis is on the location of the event; in (26b), the emphasis is on the time, and, in (26c), on the thing started. Stated in another way, (26a) answers the question, "Where did lightning start a major forest fire in 1988?"; (26b) answers the question, "When did lightning start a major forest fire in Yellowstone?"; and (26c) answers the question, "What did lightning do in Yellowstone in 1988?" or "What did lightning start in Yellowstone in 1988?" As a general rule, we can say that, in English, different emphases result from different syntactic arrangements of elements and, more specifically, that in declarative sentences unaffected by contrastive stress or any special focusing transformation (e.g., *It*-Cleft), end position is normally the emphatic position. That emphasized information falls syntactically in the same relative position as new information certainly is no accident. Prominent ideas, because of their higher information value, are (or should be) a part—or really, the "peak"—of new information.

Again, this kind of knowledge is knowledge that students already tacitly possess, as evidenced by their ability to produce (and understand) proper fragments in conversation. If teachers ask students which of the sentences in (26) most appropriately answers the question, "When did lightning start a major forest fire in Yellowstone?" students are much more likely to say (26b) rather than (26a) or

(26c). Indeed, if asked to answer the question in the most natural way, they will in all probability respond with either "in 1988" or "1988" (the latter being the peak itself). Both answers, however, indicate a conversational ability to isolate, in appropriate fragment form, the key information from less important information in the base sentence. Put in another way, writers who have the ability to produce (and understand) appropriate fragments in English conversation also have the basic tools to identify significant ideas from less significant ones in their writing, or, more in the terms developed here, significant fragments from less significant ones.

The correlation between the *wh*-questions above and their fragment answers is also no accident. It simply reflects speakers' already-acquired yet tacit knowledge of how to highlight new—and key—information in conversation by deleting given (or assumed) information. Although students who are native speakers of English do not all possess equal social skills in conversation, they are all equally skilled in their ability to produce and understand grammatical *wh*-questions and, more important here, to form corresponding and highlighted fragment answers. One easy way to make students aware of this ability (i.e., bring it to the level of consciousness) is to give students a sentence like *Lightning started a major forest fire in 1988 in Yellowstone* and ask them to form various kinds of *wh*-questions from it (e.g., *Where did lightning start a major forest fire in 1988? When did lightning start a major forest fire in Yellowstone?*), and then let them provide the answers, first in full sentence form (*Lightning started a major forest fire in 1988 in Yellowstone; Lightning started a major forest fire in Yellowstone in 1988*), then in fragment form (*in Yellowstone; in 1988*). The fragment answers will, of course, be the highlighted new information of the base sentences.

Also worthy of mention here is that, contrary to the way they actually create appropriate fragments in conversation, many students think that initial, not final, position is the emphatic position in sentences. This contradiction, however, has a plausible explanation. When students write, they tend to put to paper what first comes to mind, and what first comes to mind (and probably in fragment form) is the most salient idea, which is usually also the key or prominent idea. Hence, students will often write first what should really go last unless, of course, teachers make explicit the implicit knowledge that students actually employ in conversation. Also worth mentioning here is that, although many students (and some teachers) think proper emphasis to be of only minor importance in writing, what seems trivial initially soon adds up to a major cumulative effect. Since every sentence (unless it's completely redundant or irrelevant) contains some prominent idea, unskilled or careless writers could very well compose every sentence in a piece of writing with the wrong emphasis of ideas, with the end result being "flat writing," or writing lacking forcefulness. That sentences having proper emphasis usually create intended rhetorical effects and sentences lacking it sometimes create unintended ones, then, links closely with how information is structured in English sentences. The optimal structure is one in which given information first lays the groundwork so that ideas can build to a climax at the end of the sentence (i.e., the position of emphasis). Indeed, organizing sentences with proper emphases is, on a smaller scale, much like organizing the telling of jokes—that is, background information comes first to set up the joke; then comes the high point, or the punch line. To carry the analogy a bit further, just as a joke teller can ruin any potentially funny joke by revealing too early the punch line, so writers can ruin any potentially effective sentence—and, cumulatively, the whole essay—by revealing too early the prominent idea.

Coherence

Attention to the given-new information structure of sentences can also help teachers explain how and why good writing coheres, or sticks together. Studies consistently show that the most highly rated student essays are also the most highly rated in coherence and vice versa. Yet coherence is a difficult concept for unskilled writers to grasp, much less produce in their writing. What is just as disturbing is that coherence is equally difficult for teachers to conceptualize and present fruitfully in the classroom. Because of the attendant difficulties, teachers often avoid addressing the problem of coherence altogether, or if they do address it, they touch on only certain mechanical and cosmetic additions (e.g., the use of transitional expressions and parallel structure). These mechanical and cosmetic additions, while helpful at times, hardly get at what is most often the root of the problem, namely, the misarrangement of given and new information within and between sentences.

Take, for example, the paragraph below, in which a student writer (a college freshman) argues that all varsity teams at the school should have an accompanying junior varsity program. I believe it typifies the kind of writing that teachers receive from writers who have not yet learned to take careful heed of the given-new information structure of English sentences. While ideas expressed in the paragraph show detail and some thought, the paragraph itself does not hold together or flow well. If coherent writing stems from a sequence of given information followed by new information, we can see why the writing seems to lack coherence. To simplify matters here, I have italicized what is probably the key idea of the new information presented in each sentence. (The first sentence is assumed to carry all new information.)

> (1) At our school, the football team is one of the few teams to have *a well-organized junior varsity program.* (2) The school knows it must have *a strong j.v. team to field a strong, experienced varsity.* (3) *The women's field hockey team* is a prime example of what a strong junior varsity program can do for the varsity program. (4) *Five separate j.v. hockey teams, three of which compete against other schools,* make up the women's field hockey program. (5) The varsity finished as *the fourth best team in the nation* because of this program. (6) Over and beyond the high ranking, *over one hundred girls at the school participate in this single sport.* (7) Every sport should be *the same.*

By looking at just the key ideas italicized above, we can see that the student has spent time thinking about content. At the same time we can see from the location of some of the key ideas why the paragraph does not read very well. In sentences 3–5, the key ideas (all part of new information), are misplaced with respect to the given-plus-new sequence.

Unfortunately, this kind of mispositioning also frequently afflicts paragraphs generated by means of sentence-combining exercises. Although studies indicate that students exposed to sentence combining show real gains in writing, particularly with respect to a more varied and mature sentence style (see Hillocks 1986, 141–46, for a summary), teachers who have worked with sentence-combining exercises (especially uncued ones) can attest that the varied and complex sentences that students produce often do not connect very well with succeeding sentences. Although individual sentences may have the look of maturity and generally read well in isolation, the sentences fail to hold together satisfactorily as text because wrong elements are subordinated, elements are sequenced improperly, or both. What is usually and most obviously missing is an adherence to the given-plus-new information structure of sentences. The fault is easy enough to pinpoint. Sentence-combining exercises generally focus on the construction of syntactic form, not the construction of meaning. Because of this neglect of meaning, sentence combining does not—indeed, cannot—reach its full potential in improving writing quality.

To help deal with this neglect, teachers can easily design supplementary exercises in which students must rearrange pieces of information (i.e., fragments) to form sentences adhering to the given-plus-new sequence. Consider the sample exercise below in which students who have been introduced to the given-new sequence (and the notion of emphasis, or "key idea") are asked to rearrange the information in the asterisked items in (3–5) in order to come up with the smoothest-reading paragraph:

(1) At our school, the football team is one of the few teams to have a well-organized junior varsity program. (2) The school knows it must have a strong j.v. team to field a strong, experienced varsity. (3) */ the women's field hockey team / a prime example of / is / what a strong junior varsity program can do for the varsity program /. (4) */ five separate j.v. hockey teams / the women's field hockey program / three of which / consists of / compete against other schools /. (5) */ as the fourth best team in the nation / because of this program / the varsity finished /. (6) Over and beyond the high ranking, over one hundred girls at the school participate in this single sport. (7) Every sport should be the same.

If students pay heed to the given-plus-new sequence (and to the idea that the key idea usually goes last), they will in all likelihood come up with a revision like the following:

(1) At our school, the football team is one of the few teams to have a well-organized junior varsity program. (2) The school knows it must have a strong j.v. team to field a strong, experienced varsity. (3) A prime example of what a strong junior varsity program can do for the varsity program is the women's field hockey team. (4) The women's field hockey program consists of five separate j.v. hockey teams, three of which compete against other schools. (5) Because of this program, the varsity finished as the fourth best team in the nation. (6) Over and beyond the high ranking, over one hundred girls at the school participate in this single sport. (7) Every sport should be the same.

While the revised paragraph still has problems (e.g., a rather monotonous style), it is more coherent than the earlier version. The monotonous style can be reduced by employing in combination other devices of coherence than just the given-plus-new sequencing of information. For example, by examining the italicized key ideas of each sentence given earlier, we see that the key idea of the whole paragraph centrally concerns not the football team's junior varsity program but really the hockey team's junior varsity program as an exemplar for other varsity sports. We can reflect this focus by rewriting the first sentence as *To field strong, experienced varsity teams, our school needs a strong junior varsity program for each sport* and then continuing with the hockey team's junior varsity program as the prime example. The main point here is that while other devices for achieving coherence may prove helpful, they come after (not before) the student has laid a solid foundation with the given-plus-new sequence. Studies by Witte and Faigley (1981), Witte (1983), Vande Kopple (1982a, 1982b, 1983), and Glatt (1982) indicate that adherence to the given-new information sequence in writing improves both readability and memorability. In short, without a given-new foundation, the other devices to improve coherence are merely bandages patching up a more basic problem.

Implications for Grammar Instruction

The fact that the given-new concept helps clarify and unify a highly diverse range of writing problems has considerable implications for the teaching of grammar as a tool to improve writing. If, as research seems to indicate, formal instruction in grammar has failed to produce any significant improvement in writing (for a summary of such studies, see Braddock et al. 1963 and Hillocks 1986), the causes of this failure may lie not so much in what grammar teaches but in what it does not teach. Historically, classroom grammars, whether traditional, structural, or transformational/generative, have been essentially syntax- or form-oriented, specifically, a focus on the structure of the sentence and its parts and the rules of sentence formation. While this orientation has probably made students more aware of the syntactic form of the sentence, it has not transferred into writing improvement if we believe what research tells us.[2]

This lack of success, I would contend, has much to do with the limits of syntax-oriented grammars, particularly the failure of such grammars to relate the study of syntax to other areas of writing. If we view competent writing as an amalgam of competencies in the traditional areas of content, organization, and style, then grammar, as it is currently conceived and taught in the schools, has most to offer in the area of style (defined broadly as recurrent or characteristic linguistic forms in a text). At minimum, grammar instruction may provide a common set of terms to talk about sentences and their parts (which is considerably better than having no common terms at all). At best, grammar instruction may help students better understand the structure of sentences and the processes of sentence formation and thereby make students more aware of the systematic nature of language. In so doing, grammar study may also help students become more aware of the nature and social ramifications of nonconventional features within the sentence unit. With respect to significantly improving writing quality, however, what is grammar's greatest strength becomes its greatest weakness. The very focus on the syntactic structure of sentences ensures that grammar instruction will have much to say about the form and style of sentences but very little to say about the content and organization of writing, areas which extend beyond the borders of the sentence unit and—more significantly—count more in actually enhancing writing quality. Put in another way, because grammar, as it is presently conceived and taught, does not connect well with organization and content beyond the sentence level, it does not connect well with writing improvement. In a nutshell, grammar limits its possibilities by its too-narrow focus.

Yet what is to be done? Do we chuck the whole grammar enterprise, as many of the anti-grammar advocates have suggested? No, grammar instruction does—or, at least, should—have a place in the curriculum since it gives students a better understanding of language, its structure, and its uses. A study of these areas can be not only intellectually stimulating but also personally revealing to students as they discover more about their uniqueness as humans. (Whether this study comes best early or later is a matter of dispute, but it should come at some point.) If the primary goal, however, is writing improvement and not grammar for its own sake, then grammar instruction will need not demolition but rather some radical revamping. To make grammar instruction more productive in writing instruction, teachers will have to reduce significantly the current focus on the syntax of sentences, not because syntax is unworthy of study, but rather because syntax alone, as research seems to indicate, does not—and probably cannot—produce significant writing improvement. If we really wish to teach grammar as a tool for improving writing (as opposed to teaching grammar as an intellectual discipline), we will need not only to streamline the teaching of syntax to the bare essentials but, more important, to find ways to integrate that streamlined syntax with the teaching of content and organization. Without this integration, there is probably little hope of grammar instruction ever contributing significantly to writing improvement.

Integrating Content and Organization

I believe that the concept of given and new information discussed earlier offers one promising way to begin an integration of content and organization. If we view writing not as a creation of organized form (as conventional grammar approaches force us to do) but rather as a creation of organized meaning, we not only get a more intuitively satisfying idea of what writing is but also a clearer understanding of why an approach based on the given-new concept offers greater possibilities for connecting with writing than an approach based on syntactic constructions like "subject noun phrase" and "verb phrase." While knowing such constructions is useful, an approach focused on syntactic forms leads only to other syntactic forms, not to any easy and natural integration of content and organization of structures larger than the sentence unit (e.g., paragraph and essay), hence probably not to any significant general improvement in writing.

In contrast, an approach focused on meaning, specifically, on the given-new concept, offers more promising possibilities for integrating content. First, because given and new information are semantic/pragmatic units rather than syntactic ones, they already constitute part of the content, or meaning, of writing, as opposed to, say, noun phrases or verb phrases, which constitute part of the form of sentences. That is, given and new information require no integration with content because they are already part of content. Moreover, this content, far from being irrelevant to writing, connects vitally to the source of many kinds of content-related problems, namely, the need to establish expected background (i.e., given) information to support and clarify new information. Just as important, this content can extend beyond the borders of the sentence unit, since what is given or new information can be established in earlier or later sentences, indeed in earlier or later paragraphs. In this approach, syntactic form would not be irrelevant or unimportant, just better integrated for the purposes of writing instruction. As indicated earlier, given information tends to appear at the beginning of sentences, most frequently in subjects, and new information in predicates (i.e., verb phrases) as in, for example, direct objects. Being meaning concepts, however, given and new information cannot be uniquely defined with respect to syntactic constructions. New information may appear not only in the form of a direct object but also in the form of a subject noun phrase; similarly, while given information often appears in subject form, it may reappear later in direct object form. In sum, because given and new information are, by their nature, part of meaning, they integrate easily with the content of writing; moreover, because given and new information interact with various parts of the sentence, they also integrate easily with syntax.

The given-new concept also holds strong promise for integration with organization. Organization here, however, would not be that of syntactic elements, as in the study of conventional grammars, but rather the organization of meaning. Although linear sequencing represents the most basic form of the organization of given and new information, clearly more complex schemes can be isolated and described. If we let the symbol A represent given information and the symbol B (and also the symbols C and D) initially represent new information and then given information once it gets mentioned, the organization dealt with in the earlier examples was A + B, B + C, C + D. However, as Daneš (1974) shows, the two types of information can be—indeed are—arranged in other ways. For example, given and new information can be organized hierarchically as A + B, A + B, A + B, etc., where the given information is repeated in the same or similar phrasing at the beginning of subsequent sentences, or, alternatively, as A + B, A_1 + B, A_2 + B, A_3 + B, etc., where the given information A in subsequent sentences is broken down hierarchically into derivative subtopics (e.g., A = minorities living in California, A_1 = Hispanic Americans, A_2 = Asian Americans, A_3 = African Americans). Written texts can have various combinations of these organizational patterns, as well as more complex patterns. Markels (1984), for example, discusses organizational patterns involving "chains" of given or deducible meaning in paragraphs. The main point, however, is that given and new information are arranged into a describable structure and, hence, integrate easily with organization not only within sentences but also—and more significantly—within larger textual units such as the paragraph and the essay.

Implications for the Grammar-Writing Relationship

That an approach based on the concept of given and new information offers an easy and natural way to integrate content and organization has considerable implications for the teaching of grammar as a tool for improving writing. If it is true that content and organization are more crucial to writing quality than style and if it is also true that the teaching of syntax-oriented grammars has failed to bring significant improvement in writing primarily because such grammars do not connect well with the important areas of content and organization, then the remedy does not lie in prescribing heavier doses of these grammars. These grammars probably bring benefits in the more limited area of sentence style; however, sentence style (particularly, "sentence mechanics") is not the whole or even the most important part of good writing. Because syntax-oriented approaches fail to touch upon, much less integrate with, the content and organizational aspects of writing, such approaches are likely to produce gains that are relatively small and disproportionate to the time and effort expended.

Implementation of an approach based on the given-new concept means that we can introduce the principles and value of good organization and content at a much earlier stage in writing instruction. Indeed, teachers can begin this integration as early as the sentence level. For example, if teachers introduce some basic syntactic categories such as sentence, subject, verb, noun phrase, and modifier, they can focus on how given and new information (meaning or content) are sequenced (organized) in sentences and how a characteristic kind of organization (i.e., style) results in ease of reader comprehension. Although the writing of sentences is less complex than the writing of paragraphs or essays, the concepts and skills learned and practiced at the sentence level can have applicability at the more complex levels. Take, for example, the generation of content. If students learn on the sentence level that the understanding of new information presented in a sentence requires some given information as background (or as a transition from the preceding sentence), they have both a rationale and a guide for generating additional but necessary content. Obviously, the rationale and guide which apply at the sentence level apply at the paragraph level as well; that is, the writing of certain paragraphs first requires the establishment of given information in a previous paragraph. This link with larger structures holds also with organization. If students learn and practice on the sentence level that given information precedes new information and that the prominent idea usually comes at the end, they are, on a smaller scale, also learning about and practicing an organizational principle that applies to many kinds of paragraphs and essays. Even if students do not always transfer this knowledge gained at the sentence level to the larger structures, the early learning and practice on the sentence level should, at least, facilitate explanation and treatment at the paragraph and essay level.

Obviously, such an approach to grammar and writing calls for a different focus than that traditionally taken in the classroom. Rather than focusing exclusively on questions like, What is the subject and verb of the sentence? or, What tense is the verb? the proposed approach calls for such questions as, What is given and new information in the sentence? To whom and why? What further information is needed to make the already-stated information more understandable or convincing? Is there any stated information which is not needed? Is there a correct sequencing of given and new information? Why or why not? If not, what is the best way to organize the given and new information? What is the effect of this reorganization? Why does it produce the effect that it does? Such questions, which lie at the heart of effective communication but which often go unattended in strictly syntax-centered approaches, become the basis of instruction, discussion, and practice.

The foregoing is not to suggest that an approach focused on the given-new concept will miraculously transform students at all grade levels into instant skilled writers or that it will even solve all the writing deficiencies in one writing assignment. The approach neither is nor is meant to be a cure-all. It does, however, offer teachers a way of handling in a more unified manner a wide variety of common writing problems ranging from the graphological (e.g., semicolons, quotation marks, comma usage in relative clauses) to the syntactic (e.g., subject-verb agreement) to the semantic/pragmatic (e.g., consistency of person and number in nouns, consistency of verb tense, use of articles and pronouns, word choice, emphasis, coherence). Last but not least, the approach helps integrate more easily and more naturally the areas of content, organization, and style. The integration of these areas is encouraged and facilitated by several interlinking factors. First, the syntax of sentences, besides dealing with form, conveys meaning, or content (given and new information). Second, the effective conveyance of this meaning is connected to a specifiable sequential organization (i.e., given information followed by new information). Third, the appropriate organization of this meaning makes for a transparent style of writing which enhances readability and memorability. Fourth, all the foregoing factors concern not just the writing of effective sentences but also the writing of effective paragraphs and essays. In sum, rather than viewing the three traditional areas of writing (i.e., content, organization, and style) separately, as if they bore no relationship to one another, an approach focused on the given-new concept interrelates the three, not only in the sentence but also in structures lying beyond the borders of the sentence (e.g., the paragraph and the essay).

The Role of Grammar in Writing Instruction

Does grammar instruction really have a role to play in this approach and, more generally, in writing instruction? Yes, but it will need to be a much more selective and efficient one than that currently played. If the principal goal is to improve writing (rather than to teach grammar as an academic subject in its own right), then grammar instruction should introduce only some very basic categories like "sentence" (or "independent clause"), "subject," "verb," and "modifier." The very parsimony here accords with the decreased but proper role that grammar instruction should play in writing instruction, namely, to present only those categories and principles that have the most relevance in the enhancement of writing. Ultimately, the choice and number of these categories and principles will be determined by their utility in treating the most frequent and most socially consequential writing errors. By exercising such selectivity, teachers can forego the presentation of many, if not most, of the technical terms and concepts traditionally taught in the classroom. Moreover, to increase students' awareness of language as well as to create more time for actual writing instruction and practice, teachers should present this "bare bones" grammar by taking advantage of the already-acquired linguistic knowledge of students, the vast yet tacit knowledge that native speakers of the language bring to the classroom every day. As suggested in the opening discussion of sentence fragments, native writers possess a great deal of knowledge of their language, much more than they—or their teachers—realize or, sometimes, care to admit. Because the approach based on the given-new concept seeks to streamline grammar instruction, teachers will need to tap as much as possible this unconscious knowledge of the language, this "hidden grammar."

The role of grammar will and should differ not just in degree but also in kind. Because syntax-oriented grammars cannot, by their very design, easily and naturally interrelate style, content, and organization, they will play mostly a supplementary and supportive role to something which can, namely, the concept of given and new information. To the extent that the given-new concept effectively integrates the areas of style, content, and organization and to the extent that grammar sheds light on the given-new concept, grammar can play a useful role in writing instruction, but that role will be in the background rather than the foreground. In essence, meaning and form (i.e., syntactic form) switch places. With this radical shift in perspective, formal grammar instruction, of course, becomes less, much less, but, with respect to writing instruction and practice, less can be more—and better.

Notes

1. When working with the tag-question rule, teachers should inform students that some fragments (usually noun and adjective phrase fragments) seem to undergo tag-question formation but, in fact, do not. Consider the noun-phrase fragment in (1a) and the adjective-phrase fragment in (2a) and their seemingly corresponding tag questions in (1b) and (2b):

    1. a. A fine day.
       b. A fine day, isn't it?
    2. a. Very handsome.
       b. Very handsome, isn't he?

The added elements in the tag part of (1b) and (2b)—that is, *isn't it* and *isn't he*—clearly indicate that the source of the copied elements in the tag is not *A fine day* and *Very handsome*, respectively, but rather the genuine sentences *It is a fine day* and *He is very handsome*. If the tag-question rule is applied to these two sentences, we get the following corresponding pairs:

    3. a. It is a fine day.
       b. It is a fine day, isn't it?
    4. a. He is very handsome.
       b. He is very handsome, isn't he?

As will become evident later in the discussion, an ellipsis rule of conversation allows for the subsequent deletion of unessential or understood information (here the *It is* and the *He is*). The actual sequence of changes, then, is the following:

    5. It is a fine day → It is a fine day, isn't it? → A fine day, isn't it?
    6. He is very handsome → He is very handsome, isn't he? → Very handsome, isn't he?

The main point, again, is that the tag-question rule operates on genuine sentences and not nonsentences (e.g., fragments). Corroborating evidence that *A fine day* and *Very handsome* are not genuine sentences comes from the fact they neither undergo yes-no question formation nor fit in embedded sentence slots like "They refused to believe the idea that _____" or "It is true that _____" but genuine sentences like *It is a fine day* and *He is very handsome* satisfy such tests.

2. Better suited than syntax-based grammars for relating grammar and writing are "discourse" grammars. Unfortunately, although linguistic research in both oral and written discourse has burgeoned in the last decade, little has been done in writing discourse-based pedagogical grammars. For a scope of the field of discourse analysis, see Stubbs (1983) or Brown and Yule (1983). For a more technical study focused specifically on written discourse, see DeBeaugrande (1984b).

6 The Paradoxes of Grammar Instruction

Reason has always existed, but not always in a reasonable form.

—Karl Marx

To endure the unendurable is true endurance.

—Japanese proverb

In the last two decades, probably no type of traditional instruction in the schools has been beset by as many bewildering paradoxes as formal grammar instruction. By "paradoxes," I do not mean the classical self-contradictory semantic paradoxes such as "rules having exceptions" or people "thinking the unthinkable" or even Groucho Marx's refusing to join any club agreeing to have him as a member. The kind of paradoxes I have in mind here trace their roots to neither Zeno, Zen, nor Zeppo's brother; rather, they have more conspicuously to do with inconsistencies of belief and fact or inconsistencies of saying and doing—or more conveniently, pragmatic paradoxes. Some of these paradoxes (along with causes and possible suggestions for resolution) have already emerged in the course of this study; others have appeared only implicitly. Whether explicitly or implicitly expressed, these paradoxes deserve careful attention by anyone seeking a more productive relationship between grammar and writing. As the end is, paradoxically, also the beginning, I will simply restate, in question form, the most salient of these pragmatic paradoxes and, for each, offer or recapitulate a plausible response.

1. Why are minor surface errors major errors to so many of the educated public?

By and large, the "minor surface errors" in writing (i.e., nonstandard, or unconventional, features of writing) are not intrinsically wrong, just as the conventional or standard replacements are not intrinsically right. If nonstandard features are errors at all, they are errors of usage (i.e., using forms inappropriate to the situation), not errors of inherent form. Why these minor errors become major ones to many lies ultimately in two factors. First, most readers are not trained evaluators of writing and, hence, do not always make the best judges of writing quality. Their criteria for good or bad writing may, in fact, differ considerably from those of skillfully trained composition teachers. Unable to pinpoint the exact causes of bad—or good—writing, untrained evaluators are inevitably forced to base their judgments of writing quality solely on surface stylistic features (e.g., capitalization, punctuation, spelling, use of *different from* vs. *different than*), with the consequence that these minor surface features become greatly magnified with respect to other and probably more important indicators of writing quality (e.g., content and organization). Second, like other primates of the animal kingdom, humans seek, in one way or another, to signal, enhance, and, ultimately, protect status. (Note, for example, the often painstaking care we take in the purchase, display, and maintenance of clothes, cars, and abodes, a care sometimes far exceeding the original utilitarian purposes of these artifacts.) Language partakes in these activities insofar as linguistic form conveys not just cognitive meaning but often social status as well—high, low, in between, insider, outsider. People usually gauge the status of speakers (and writers) by socially and culturally determined surface criteria. Japanese speakers, for example, gauge it principally by the presence of polite forms; British English speakers, principally by pronunciation; American English speakers, principally by "grammar." Whether we care to admit it or not, American English speakers employ various grammatical shibboleths (e.g., use of *ain't, brung*, double negatives) not only to affirm their current status within a social group but sometimes also to distance themselves from other social groups. In this reckoning of status, language features that are perfectly normal and acceptable within one group may be abnormal and unacceptable—indeed, stigmatized—by others outside the group. If so, minor surface errors may again acquire much greater significance than they actually possess, especially to evaluators who stand outside the group and who wish to signal, enhance, or protect their own status or the status of their group. Professionals (teachers included) who engage excessively in "error hunting" of surface features are particularly prone to fall into this latter group. Since language users throughout the world engage in the signaling, enhancing, and protecting of status, in both linguistic and nonlinguistic activities, we should not be overly surprised to find the same in the United States. Yet, ironically, in a country which, at its conception, supposedly eschewed the creation of social distinctions, we find what we historically sought to avoid in the very language varieties with which we speak and write.

Without question, the social status of a language variety is intimately linked to the social status of its users. As history clearly shows, the acceptance of a language variety and its conventions of use can change with changes in the social order (note, for example, the decline of French and the ascendancy of English in both public and nonpublic documents in the late Middle English period and the subsequent rise of the East Midland dialect in England). As the social status of users rises, so rises the status of the language varieties (and the nonstandard forms) they use. The social status of a group (and the individuals within the group) can rise in two ways: (1) by the social or political rise of the group itself or (2) by the social or political fall of other groups. In either case (or a combination of both), the language variety spoken by the ascendant group moves up the social ladder. In the end, what is socially prestigious, or "correct," in (formal) writing depends on which social variety of language, officially or unofficially, gains acceptance within public institutions.

2. If surface errors really are minor and superficial, why do teachers find it such a major undertaking to eliminate them?

If the unconventional writing features are dialect-influenced features, some students may not know the standard forms. In other cases, students may resist attempts to eliminate the dialect features because the features represent an integral and intimate part of their language and culture. To extend a metaphor of the oral cavity, if people are what they eat, they are also what they speak.

When dialect-influenced features are not directly involved, the causes become harder to pinpoint. Some of the causes probably lie in the workings of large-scale forces, one being the growing influence of oral culture and the accompanying decline of writing. As people read less and less, they have less and less exposure to the conventions of writing. Thus, the conventions of writing (as opposed to those of speech) often go unnoticed and must be taught formally in the schools. It stands to reason that the more conventions that have to be taught, the less attention that each particular convention receives, and, eventually, the less each is learned. On the other side of the coin, the more people become influenced by oral culture, the more the conventions of speech permeate into written discourse. Hence the greater frequency of looser organization, colloquial wording, fragments, and, generally, the less attention to precision and detail. What gets repeated frequently in oral discourse gains not only easier entry into written discourse but also continual reinforcement once there.

From a pedagogical standpoint, the primary reason for the difficulty of treatment lies in the interlinked nature of language. To teach one grammatical category, teachers must often teach many. For example, to eliminate sentence fragments from their writing, students must understand what constitutes a sentence (or independent clause), but to understand what constitutes a sentence, they must understand what constitutes a subject and a predicate. In order to understand the latter two concepts, they need some notion of noun phrase and verb, and on it goes. In other words, to teach one relevant grammatical category, teachers must often teach many, none of which are easy to grasp and any one of which, if inadequately learned, lends confusion to the whole chain of categories. The approach outlined in this study, that of relying on native students' unconscious underlying knowledge of the language, not only circumvents this frustrating chain of interlinked grammatical categories but also frees up more time for other and more important writing activities.

3. If native students have an underlying syntactic knowledge of English, why do they write with fragments, run-ons, and comma splices?

Even though native speakers possess an unconscious underlying knowledge governing sentence formation in English, they may write with fragments, run-ons, and comma splices for at least two reasons. First, they may make such errors simply because they do not yet fully understand the conventions unique to writing (as opposed to speech). For instance, although fragments are accepted in daily conversation, they are not so readily accepted in writing, particularly in formal writing. Run-ons and comma splices may reflect an unfamiliarity with graphological conventions (specifically, the use of end punctuation to mark sentence boundaries) rather than a lack of knowledge about where one sentence ends and the next one begins. This becomes all the more evident when we consider that students who write with run-ons and comma splices never "talk" with them in daily conversation. As the approach described in this study makes clear, students who write with fragments, run-ons, and comma splices demonstrate an underlying knowledge of what a sentence is by their ability in daily conversation to form proper tag questions and yes-no questions, two operations which presuppose an understanding of what constitutes a sentence. When applied to word sequences, the tag- and yes-no question rules work properly only with genuine sentences, not with nonsentences. Because native speakers of English already unconsciously know how the tag- and yes-no question rules operate, they do not need to be taught the operations, but they can benefit if they learn how to exploit the two rules as a means of verifying the sentencehood of doubtful sequences.

Second, native writers who write with fragments, run-ons, and comma splices may do so for the same reasons they make other kinds of writing errors: that is, from inattention, carelessness, laziness, etc. Although native writers already possess the requisite ability to produce genuine sentences of the language, they may, nonetheless, produce fragments, run-ons, and comma splices because they either do not apply that ability or apply it incorrectly. Either case may result in unintentional fragments, run-ons, or comma splices. We need to separate linguistic competence (i.e., the underlying knowledge of a language) from linguistic performance (i.e., the actual use or, as the case may be, the disuse or misuse of linguistic competence). Two analogies may help clarify matters here. We may stumble when walking or stammer when talking, but these mishaps do not negate our underlying knowledge of how to walk and how to talk. So it is with native students' underlying knowledge of the formation of genuine sentences.

4. If native students already possess an underlying knowledge of the grammar of sentences, and if written discourse consists of sequences of sentences, why is it that many still cannot write well?

There is little reason to believe that the ability to write grammatical— and even prescriptively correct—sentences will ensure good writing. Written discourse may consist of sequences of sentences, but it also encompasses much more; it is certainly more than a "grammar of sentences." For one thing, sentences in good writing exhibit not only appropriate form (which grammar instruction might help improve) but also appropriate content (which grammar instruction usually cannot improve to any great extent). Stated in a slightly different way, students can write much but actually say little if the content is irrelevant or inaccurate; conversely, they can write little and say much if the content is on the button. Yet even the addition of appropriate content will not result in good writing if that content is not properly organized, both within and between sentences. Written discourse consists of not merely sequences of sentences but sequences of organized information, or content. The sentences that students compose, no matter how grammatically and stylistically impeccable, cannot be randomly arranged. More specifically, the given and new information contained in sentences must logically and efficiently connect to the information contained or assumed in prior sentences. Unskilled native writers, though possessing an underlying knowledge of sentence formation, often fail to make these connections clear. More unfortunate, perhaps, grammar instruction, as it is presently conceived and presented, expends a disproportionate amount of time on matters of syntactic form (the structure of the sentence and its parts), little time on the larger and more crucial areas of content and discourse organization, and even less time on the integration of style, content, and organization.

5. Why does formal grammar instruction help some students become better writers but not others; or, alternatively, why did formal grammar instruction make me a better writer but not many of my students?

Good writing requires a host of integrated skills in the three major areas of content, organization, and style. As presently conceived and taught, grammar (i.e., sentence grammar) has little to offer in the areas of content and organization and most to offer in the area of style. Of these three areas, however, content and organization are probably much more crucial to writing quality than is style. Writing that is weak in style but strong in content and organization can still be passably adequate (the basic material is, at least, there for refinement); however, writing that is strong in style but weak in content and organization can hardly be judged as equal in writing quality. That is, it seems stranger to say, "Although this student's writing is weak in content and organization, it is still good writing," than to say, "Although this student's writing is weak in style, it is still good writing." If grammar instruction has most to offer in the area of style but very little to offer in the areas of content and organization, then it follows that students whose writing is weak in the latter two areas will have much less of a chance of making significant gains in writing quality through grammar instruction alone; conversely, students whose writings exhibit competence in content and organization but weaknesses in style can conceivably profit from formal grammar instruction, provided, of course, that instruction focuses on the stylistic weaknesses. Yet even in the more restricted area of style (as opposed to writing in general), variances occur in writing improvement. Some students may profit greatly from formal grammar instruction and some not at all. The difficulty of the subject matter and student motivation are, of course, influencing factors here. Those who learn the concepts and principles—and more important, skillfully apply them in their writing—will obviously profit more than those who neither learn nor apply them.

Paradoxically, sometimes even students who fail to learn the concepts and principles adequately or who have never been exposed to formal grammar instruction still show competency in style. My guess here is that such students acquire not only a better sense of the differing conventions between writing and speech but, more generally, an intuitive feel for style (both in the descriptive and prescriptive sense) on the basis of conscientious outside reading. This intuitive feel, I would contend, involves viewing and analyzing written discourse in ways different from lesser skilled writers.

6. Why do teachers continue formal grammar instruction when most research indicates that it does not produce significant writing improvement?

This question probably represents the most paradoxical of all the paradoxes concerning grammar instruction. The source of this pragmatic paradox may ultimately lie in the rigidity of writing programs themselves, in which case it involves not just teachers but also administrators and curriculum planners as well. Indeed, given the regimentation of many writing programs, including the use of standardized grammar texts and examinations, teachers may have little say in the matter at all. Comments here, however, will be restricted to teachers, not because they are necessarily the sole or even the chief creators of the paradox but because they operate on the front lines of grammar instruction and are usually the ones held most directly accountable for the success or failure of writing instruction.

Why teachers continue to teach formal grammar despite the research findings probably lies in several factors, the three most plausible ones being the following:

1. Teachers are unaware of current research.
2. Teachers are aware of current research but don't really believe it.
3. Teachers are aware of current research and believe it but have nothing better to offer in the place of formal grammar instruction.

The first factor seems highly plausible in light of the heavy workload of teachers, the lack of easy access to research libraries, and the general lack of funds for teacher training and development. It stands to reason that the less free time and the less financial and resource support available, the less opportunity (and eventually, less incentive) teachers will have to keep abreast in their fields. Put in bald, practical terms, teachers cannot implement research findings if they have little or no access to the findings.

The second factor, that teachers are aware of the current research but disbelieve it, may, however, be just as influential in the continuance of formal grammar instruction as a means of writing improvement. A considerable number of teachers believe that, if grammar instruction worked for them in improving their writing, it must also work for their students (but see the response to Question 5 in the previous section). Other teachers, particularly those who themselves have invested great time and effort in learning the complexities of grammar and in refining their techniques of grammar instruction, believe that the research itself has somehow gone astray, that it focused on the wrong students—or the wrong teachers—with imprecise and fallible experimental procedures, or that the research has become politicized or stained with faddism, or that the research represents the conspiratorial and nefarious doings of anti-grammar forces seeking to eliminate what they once dreaded to study. Whether accurate or not, these beliefs reveal, if anything, a strong loyalty to traditional grammar instruction and perhaps an equally strong skepticism of the research findings in writing. Given the pervasiveness and strength of the beliefs here, changes in methods and focus seem to require far more than the results of empirical studies.

The third factor, that teachers believe the current research but know of nothing better to offer in the place of formal grammar instruction, may constitute the most powerful force in the continuance of formal grammar instruction. Given the fact that, for many teachers, grammar instruction has occupied a significant part of writing instruction, what does one do if formal instruction in grammar is suddenly dropped? What will fill the black hole?

As suggested by this study, teachers do not have to abandon grammar, but if the chief goal is writing improvement and not grammar for its own sake, grammar instruction will have to be much more selective and much more cost-efficient than in the past. This means not only limiting the scope of grammar instruction to only those categories and principles which elucidate the most frequent and serious writing problems but also exploiting as much as possible students' already-acquired knowledge of the language. Just as important, teachers will need to integrate this minimal set of categories and principles, or "writer's grammar," with content and organization, two crucial areas that syntax-based grammars leave virtually untouched. Without this integration, grammar study stands very little chance of enhancing writing quality in any significant way. This study suggests that the integration can be most easily and naturally accomplished not by a syntactic perspective but by a semantic/pragmatic one, more specifically, by means of the concept of given and new information. This shift in perspective will not lead to grammar being banished from the curriculum, but it will result in grammar playing a less dominant and more efficient role in writing instruction. To remedy certain kinds of stylistic errors, students will probably always need to have a working knowledge of a minimal set of grammatical concepts (e.g., sentence, subject, verb), but these will be taught as part of a streamlined writer's grammar and not as grammar for its own sake.

What can the teachers who now teach grammar formally gain in all this? Less time spent on formal grammar instruction will mean less time spent on preparing grammar lessons and fewer classroom hours spent on implementing and correcting tedious, mechanical exercises that most students inevitably grow to hate. Less time spent on formal grammar instruction will mean more time to spend on the frequent and most serious kinds of stylistic problems, more time to examine the various social uses and users of English, and more time to explore the power, the responsibilities, and the social ramifications accompanying the written word. It will also mean more time to explore and utilize the unconscious underlying knowledge of language that all native writers share, more time to present and explain matters of content and organization, more time to teach and engage students in the writing process, and, of course, more time for actual writing. Less formal instruction in grammar will, furthermore, mean more time for students to find out how language makes them uniquely human, how language not only divides human beings but also unites them. In general, less formal instruction in grammar will mean more time to develop in students a healthy awareness and appreciation of language and its uses, not just of limits but also of possibilities.

In the end, less is more.

Works Cited

Anderson, Edward. 1981. Language and Success. *College English* 43:807–17.

Bamberg, Betty. 1977. Periods Are Basic: A Strategy for Eliminating Comma Faults and Run-on Sentences. In *Classroom Practices in Teaching English 1977–1978: Teaching the Basics—Really!*, edited by Ouida Clapp and the Committee on Classroom Practices. Urbana, Ill.: National Council of Teachers of English.

Beauregard-Vasquez, Linda. 1989. The USK Alternative to Traditional Grammar Instruction: A Case Study of Student Writers at A.V.C. Unpublished ms.

Bereiter, Carl, Siegfried Engelman, Jean Osborn, and Philip A. Reidford. 1966. An Academically Oriented Pre-School for Culturally Deprived Children. In *Pre-School Education Today*, edited by Fred M. Hechinger. New York: Doubleday.

Bernstein, Basil, editor. 1971. *Class, Codes and Control.* Vol. 1, *Theoretical Studies towards a Sociology of Language.* London: Routledge and Kegan Paul.

Bolton, W. F. 1982. *A Living Language.* New York: Random House.

Braddock, Richard, Richard Lloyd-Jones, and Lowell Schoer. 1963. *Research in Written Composition.* Champaign, Ill.: National Council of Teachers of English.

Brosnahan, Irene Teoh. 1976. A Few Good Words for the Comma Splice. *College English* 38:184–88.

Brown, Gillian, and George Yule. 1983. *Discourse Analysis.* Cambridge: Cambridge University Press.

Chafe, Wallace L. 1979. The Flow of Thought and the Flow of Language. In *Discourse and Syntax*, edited by T. Givón. Syntax and Semantics 12. New York: Academic Press.

Chomsky, Noam. 1965. *Aspects of the Theory of Syntax.* Cambridge: MIT Press.

———. 1959. Review of B. F. Skinner's *Verbal Behavior. Language* 35:26–58.

Christensen, Francis. 1968. The Problem of Defining a Mature Style. *English Journal* 57: 572–79.

Clark, Herbert H., and Susan E. Haviland. 1977. Comprehension and the Given-New Contract. In *Discourse Production and Comprehension*, edited by Roy O. Freedle. Advances in Discourse Processes 1. Norwood, N.J.: Ablex.

Connors, Robert J., and Andrea A. Lunsford. 1988. Frequency of Formal Errors in Current College Writing, or Ma and Pa Kettle Do Research. *College Composition and Communication* 39:395–409.

Cordeiro, Patricia. 1988. Children's Punctuation: An Analysis of Errors in Period Placement. *Research in the Teaching of English* 22:62–74.

Daneš, Frantisek. 1974. Functional Sentence Perspective and the Organization of the Text. In *Papers on Functional Sentence Perspective*, edited by Frantisek Daneš. The Hague: Mouton.

Davis, Frederica. 1984. In Defense of Grammar. *English Education* 16:151–64.

DeBeaugrande, Robert. 1984a. Forward to the Basics: Getting Down to Grammar. *College Composition and Communication* 35:358–67.

———. 1984b. *Text Production: Toward a Science of Composition*. Advances in Discourse Processes 11. Norwood, N.J.: Ablex.

DeBoer, John J. 1959. Grammar in Language Teaching. *Elementary English* 36:413–21.

D'Eloia, Sarah. 1977. The Uses—and Limits—of Grammar. *Journal of Basic Writing* 1(3): 1–48.

Elley, W. B., I. H. Barham, H. Lamb, and M. Wyllie. 1976. The Role of Grammar in a Secondary School English Curriculum. *Research in the Teaching of English* 10:5–21.

Falk, Julia S. 1979. Language Acquisition and the Teaching and Learning of Writing. *College English* 41:436–47.

Firbas, Jan. 1986. On the Dynamics of Written Communication in the Light of the Theory of Functional Sentence Perspective. In *Studying Writing: Linguistic Approaches*, edited by Charles R. Cooper and Sidney Greenbaum. Beverly Hills, Calif.: Sage.

———. 1974. Some Aspects of the Czechoslovak Approach to Problems of Functional Sentence Perspective. In *Papers on Functional Sentence Perspective*, edited by Frantisek Daneš. The Hague: Mouton.

Fischer, John L. 1958. Social Influences on the Choice of a Linguistic Variant. *Word* 14:47–56.

Flower, Linda. 1979. Writer-Based Prose: A Cognitive Basis for Problems in Writing. *College English* 41:19–37.

Francis, W. Nelson. 1954. Revolution in Grammar. *Quarterly Journal of Speech* 40:299–312.

Givón, T. 1989. *Mind, Code and Context: Essays in Pragmatics*. Hillsdale, N.J.: Erlbaum.

Glatt, Barbara S. 1982. Defining Thematic Progressions and Their Relationship to Reader Comprehension. In *What Writers Know: The Language, Process, and Structure of Written Discourse*, edited by Martin Nystrand. New York: Academic Press.

Hairston, Maxine. 1981. Not All Errors Are Created Equal: Nonacademic Readers in the Professions Respond to Lapses in Usage. *College English* 43:794–806.

Harris, Muriel. 1981. Mending the Fragmented Free Modifier. *College Composition and Communication* 32:175–82.

Hartwell, Patrick. 1985. Grammar, Grammars, and the Teaching of Grammar. *College English* 47:105–27.

Haviland, Susan E., and Herbert H. Clark. 1974. What's New? Acquiring New Information as a Process in Comprehension. *Journal of Verbal Learning and Verbal Behavior* 13:512–21.

Hillocks, George, Jr. 1986. *Research on Written Composition: New Directions for Teaching.* Urbana, Ill.: ERIC Clearinghouse on Reading and Communication Skills and the National Conference on Research in English.

Holt, J. R. 1982. In Defense of Formal Grammar. *Curriculum Review* 21:173–78.

Hoyt, Franklin S. 1906. The Place of Grammar in the Elementary Curriculum. *Teachers College Record* 7:467–500.

Jespersen, Otto. [1909–49] 1961. *A Modern English Grammar on Historical Principles.* Reprint. 7 vols. London: George Allen and Unwin.

Kline, Charles R., Jr., and W. Dean Memering. 1977. Formal Fragments: The English Minor Sentence. *Research in the Teaching of English* 11:97–110.

Kolln, Martha. 1981. Closing the Books on Alchemy. *College Composition and Communication* 32:139–51.

Labov, William. 1972. *Sociolinguistic Patterns.* Philadelphia: University of Pennsylvania Press.

———. 1969. The Logic of Nonstandard English. In *Georgetown University 20th Annual Round Table.* Monograph Series on Languages and Linguistics 22. Washington, D.C.: Georgetown University Press. (Also in *Language in the Inner City: Studies in the Black English Vernacular,* by William Labov. Philadelphia: University of Pennsylvania Press, 1972.)

Lakoff, Robin Tolmach. 1982. Some of My Favorite Writers Are Literate: The Mingling of Oral and Literate Strategies in Written Communication. In *Spoken and Written Language: Exploring Orality and Literacy,* edited by Deborah Tannen. Advances in Discourse Processes 9. Norwood, N.J.: Ablex.

Lenneberg, Eric H. 1967. *Biological Foundations of Language.* New York: John Wiley and Sons.

Levine, Lewis, and Harry J. Crockett, Jr. 1966. Speech Variations in a Piedmont Community. *Sociological Inquiry* 36:204–26. (Also in *A Various Language,* edited by Juanita V. Williamson and Virginia M. Burke. New York: Holt, 1971.)

Markels, Robin Bell. 1984. *A New Perspective on Cohesion in Expository Paragraphs.* Carbondale: Southern Illinois University Press.

McNeill, David. 1970. *The Acquisition of Language: The Study of Developmental Psycholinguistics.* New York: Harper and Row.

Meckel, Henry C. 1963. Research on Teaching Composition and Literature. In *Handbook of Research on Teaching,* edited by N. L. Gage. Chicago: Rand McNally.

Morgan, J. L. 1973. Sentence Fragments and the Notion "Sentence." *Issues in Linguistics: Papers in Honor of Henry and Renée Kahane,* edited by Braj B. Kachru, Robert B. Lees, Yakov Malkiel, Angelina Pietrangeli, and Sol Saporta. Urbana: University of Illinois Press.

Neuleib, Janice. 1977. The Relation of Formal Grammar to Composition. *College Composition and Communication* 28:247–50.

Neuleib, Janice, and Irene Brosnahan. 1987. Teaching Grammar to Writers. *Journal of Basic Writing* 6(1): 28–35.

Noguchi, Rei R. 1987. Transformational-Generative Syntax and the Teaching of Sentence Mechanics. *Journal of Basic Writing* 6(2): 26–36.

Ong, Walter J. 1944. Historical Backgrounds of Elizabethan and Jacobean Punctuation Theory. *PMLA* 59:349–60.

Parris, P. B. n.d. Sisyphus and the Comma Splice. *Temple University Working Papers in Composition*. Philadelphia: Temple University.

Prince, Ellen F. 1981. Toward a Taxonomy of Given-New Information. In *Radical Pragmatics*, edited by Peter Cole. New York: Academic Press.

Quirk, Randolph, Sidney Greenbaum, Geoffrey Leech, and Jan Svartvik. 1985. *A Comprehensive Grammar of the English Language*. London: Longman.

Sanborn, Jean. 1986. Grammar: Good Wine before Its Time. *English Journal* 75(March): 72–80.

Shaughnessy, Mina P. 1977. *Errors and Expectations*. New York: Oxford University Press.

Shuy, Roger W. 1973. Language and Success: Who Are the Judges? In *Varieties of Present-Day English*, edited by Richard W. Bailey and Jay L. Robinson. New York: Macmillan.

Shuy, Roger W., Walter A. Wolfram, and William K. Riley. 1967. *Linguistic Correlates of Social Stratification in Detroit Speech*. Washington, D.C.: U.S. Office of Education. Final Report, Project 6-1347.

Sloan, Gary. 1979. The Subversive Effects of an Oral Culture on Student Writing. *College Composition and Communication* 30:156–60.

Stubbs, Michael. 1983. *Discourse Analysis: The Sociolinguistic Analysis of Natural Language*. Chicago: University of Chicago Press.

Sutton, Gary A. 1976. Do We Need to Teach a Grammar Terminology? *English Journal* 65(December): 37–40.

Tabbert, Russell. 1984. Parsing the Question "Why Teach Grammar?" *English Journal* 73(March): 38–42.

Trudgill, Peter. 1972. Sex, Covert Prestige and Linguistic Change in the Urban British English of Norwich. *Language in Society* 1:179–95.

Vande Kopple, William J. 1982a. Functional Sentence Perspective, Composition, and Reading. *College Composition and Communication* 33:50–63.

—. 1982b. The Given-New Strategy of Comprehension and Some Natural Expository Paragraphs. *Journal of Psycholinguistic Research* 11: 501–20.

—. 1983. Something Old, Something New: Functional Sentence Perspective. *Research in the Teaching of English* 17: 85–99.

Wardhaugh, Ronald. 1985. *How Conversation Works*. Oxford: Basil Blackwell.

Witte, Stephen P. 1983. Topical Structure and Revision: An Exploratory Study. *College Composition and Communication* 34:313–41.

Witte, Stephen P., and Lester Faigley. 1981. Coherence, Cohesion, and Writing Quality. *College Composition and Communication* 32:189–204.

Author

Rei R. Noguchi, associate professor of English at California State University, Northridge, teaches courses in linguistics in the Department of English and in the Linguistics Interdisciplinary Program. He received his Ph.D. in English with a specialization in English language and linguistics from Indiana University, Bloomington. He has published articles in such journals as *International Review of Applied Linguistics, Studies in Philology, Language and Style, Journal of Literary Semantics, Lingua e Stile, Journal of Beckett Studies*, and *Journal of Basic Writing*. His interests include linguistic stylistics, semantics and pragmatics, historical linguistics, and applications of linguistics to writing.